Embracing the Law

PROCEEDINGS of the
MORMON THEOLOGY SEMINAR

THE PROCEEDINGS OF THE MORMON THEOLOGY SEMINAR
series is based on a novel idea: that Mormons do theology. Doing theology is different from weighing history or
deciding doctrine. Theology speculates. It experiments
with questions and advances hypotheses. It tests new
angles and pulls loose threads.

The Mormon Theology Seminar organizes interdisciplin-
ary, collaborative, theological readings of Latter-day Saint
scripture. Seminar participants with diverse backgrounds
closely explore familiar texts in creative ways. In partner-
ship with the Laura F. Willes Center for Book of Mormon
Studies at the Neal A. Maxwell Institute for Religious
Scholarship, the Mormon Theology Seminar presents
these experiments upon the word to foster greater theological engagement with basic Mormon texts.

Series Editor

Brian M. Hauglid

Other MORMON THEOLOGY SEMINAR *books include:*

Adam S. Miller, ed.,
An Experiment on the Word: Reading Alma 32

Joseph M. Spencer and Jenny Webb, eds.,
Reading Nephi Reading Isaiah: 2 Nephi 26–27

Julie M. Smith, ed.,
Apocalypse: Reading Revelation 21–22

mi.byu.edu/pmts

Embracing the Law

Reading Doctrine and Covenants 42

Edited by
Jeremiah John
Joseph M. Spencer

NEAL A. MAXWELL
INSTITUTE *for*
RELIGIOUS SCHOLARSHIP

Brigham Young University
Provo, Utah

A Proceedings of the Mormon Theology Seminar book

Neal A. Maxwell Institute, Provo 84602 | maxwellinstitute.byu.edu

Library of Congress Cataloging-in-Publication Data

Names: Mormon Theology Seminar (2010 : Buena Vista, Va.), author. | John, Jeremiah, editor. | Spencer, Joseph M., editor. | Mormon Theology Seminar. Proceedings of the Mormon Theology Seminar.
Title: Embracing the law : reading Doctrine and Covenants 42 / edited by Jeremiah John and Joseph M. Spencer.
Description: Provo, Utah : Neal A. Maxwell Institute, Brigham Young University, [2017] | Series: Proceedings of the Mormon Theology Seminar | Includes bibliographical references.
Identifiers: LCCN 2017010322| ISBN 9780842530033 (print : alk. paper) | ISBN 9780842530071 (ePub) | ISBN 9780842530088 (kindle)
Subjects: LCSH: Doctrine and Covenants. Section 42--Congresses. | Church of Jesus Christ of Latter-day Saints--Doctrines--Congresses. | Mormon Church--Doctrines--Congresses.
Classification: LCC BX8628 .M67 2010 | DDC 289.3/23--dc23
LC record available at https://lccn.loc.gov/2017010322

♾ This paper meets the requirements of ANSI/NISO z39.48-1992 (Permanence of Paper).

ISBN 978-0-8425-3003-3

Cover image: Alicia Jo McMahan

Cover and book design: Jenny Webb and Andrew Heiss

Printed in the United States of America

Contents

Introduction

SECTION 42 OF THE DOCTRINE AND COVENANTS purports to be something momentous. It claims to present nothing less than God's revelation of his law to his people—a law meant to bring about the gathering of Israel, the establishment of the New Jerusalem, and the preparation of the church for the second coming of Christ. Any serious consideration of this fresh revelation of law should therefore raise the question of the general significance of divine law in the Christian world. For many Christians, the gospel of salvation is emphatically *not* a revelation of law but a revelation of grace. Other Christians, such as Catholics, understand grace as a part of the new law of Christ, but for them this new law revealed in Christ is the last and final law; no further law should be revealed between the time of Christ and the final judgment. Thus section 42 of the Doctrine and Covenants makes Mormonism stand apart from the Christian tradition, setting forth something novel in its announcement of a *new* revelation of divine law.

As is customary in publications of the Mormon Theology Seminar, we open this volume with a summary report of our collaborative findings. Each project sponsored by the seminar generates a handful of guiding questions, focal points of interest that help to direct joint study of the text under investigation. As collaborative work on the text comes to a conclusion, the contributors to the project jointly author a short summary of the sorts of answers, if any, they have discovered along the way of their research. Immediately following this introduction, the reader can find preliminary answers to the questions that drove our discussions. The summary report of course cannot convey the richness of our months of textual analysis, but it provides at least a general sense for the kinds of things we discussed. Perhaps more usefully, it also provides a basic orientation for the remainder of the book. It lays out a number of textual, historical, and theological data points that this book's several essays use again and again.

A few words might be useful by way of introducing the several essays in this volume as well. The subjects of the essays, although they are all rooted in close study of Doctrine and Covenants 42, range widely.

Nathan Oman's essay, "'I Will Give unto You My Law': Section 42 as a Legal Text and the Paradoxes of Divine Law," appears first in this collection. Oman draws on his training as a legal scholar to assess the peculiar status of Doctrine and Covenants 42 as law. Placing the revelation in a longer history of differing conceptions of divine law, he especially focuses on the complicated relationship between any divine law and the many systems of human law with which divine law might come into conflict. He argues that D&C 42 displays many features common to legal texts but also that it reveals a series of paradoxes or tensions as it carves out a unique relationship to secular law. In the end, he insists that the Doctrine and Covenants ultimately makes what might appear to outsiders as a series of historical accommodations to nondivine law into a direct feature of divine law.

In "'That My Covenant People May Be Gathered in One': The Law of Section 42 of the Doctrine and Covenants," Jeremiah John also attempts to understand the status of D&C 42 as law. But rather than putting the revelation's claim to be law into the larger historical context of a conversation about the tangle of divine and secular law, John asks how the revelation might speak to the longstanding conversation in Christian history regarding the fulfillment of law and advent of grace. Framing these questions in terms of political theology, he suggests that the Doctrine and Covenants, like passages in the Book of Mormon and occasionally in the Bible, outlines the possibility of a higher law, one that outstrips law's natural tendency to condemn and to cut off, rather than to redeem. Key to John's reading is a Thomist notion that allows for a reconciliation of law and grace through a divinely granted orientation to the good. This allows him to interpret the use of the ambiguous auxiliary verb *shall* as it is used in the law of D&C 42.

After these first two essays address themselves to the question of law, Karen Spencer turns her attention to a rather different feature of Doctrine and Covenants 42, focusing on what it has to say about the task of teaching in an ideal community. In "Teaching in Zion," she investigates the injunction in the revelation to teach by the Spirit—and especially *not* to teach if the Spirit is not received. Drawing on numerous related revelations in the Doctrine and Covenants (especially sections 20, 46, and 50), as well as on direct echoes of the Book of Mormon (and in particular of Moroni), Spencer argues that D&C 42's instructions regarding teaching should be understood as part of a larger attempt on God's part to organize the Latter-day Saint community around Spirit-driven meetings. This was, it seems, in direct response to a fraught culture of charismatic enthusiasm that had developed in Kirtland, Ohio, in the years immediately preceding the arrival of Mormonism there. Spencer shows that the response to this situation was careful and deliberate and that there remains much to learn from it.

In his contribution, "'Thou Wilt Remember the Poor': Social Justice and a Radical Reading of 'The Laws of the Church of Christ' (Doctrine and Covenants 42)," Russell Arben Fox looks at how D&C 42 might be profitably placed in conversation with the social justice tradition developed in Catholic and Reformed Christian circles. While traditional attempts to interpret the political ramifications of the law of consecration tend to contrast it with secular socialism, Fox forcefully traces the relevance of the basic commitments of the social justice tradition to the basic concerns of the revealed law of the Doctrine and Covenants. Focusing in particular on three commitments of the social justice tradition—producing a rough economic equality of persons, understanding persons as inextricably contextualized by community, and privileging those most economically compromised by current social conditions—he shows that these concerns are amply present in D&C 42. Illuminatingly, he shows that revisions made to the revelation between 1831 and 1835 tend to strengthen rather than to weaken these connections.

Robert Couch similarly focuses on the need to make D&C 42's call for the assistance of the poor particularly relevant in a contemporary context. In "Consecration, Holy War, and the Poor: An Apocalyptic Approach to Doctrine and Covenants 42," he draws on the biblical genre of apocalypse to highlight the way in which the work of reading scripture requires a change in the reader's view of the world—something particularly relevant if the poor are to be redeemed. For Couch, the apocalyptic tradition reprises still more ancient attempts to determine the boundary between Zion-like communities and "the world," and in this sense it assists in determining the meaning of the law divinely given to the early Mormon community. At the same time, he argues that the modern law of consecration represents a certain transformation of ancient Israelite notions of consecration—those bound up with the Israelite Holy War tradition—in part because the boundaries between Zion communities and the secular world are murkier today than in the ancient world. In the end, Couch calls for a full embrace of consecration in the deepest sense, transcending merely economic and ultimately pragmatist motivations because it is driven by the divine guarantee of fulfilled promises.

Finally, in a more telescoped view of the text of Doctrine and Covenants 42, Joseph M. Spencer's "Remnants of Revelation: On the Canonical Reading of Doctrine and Covenants 42" concludes this volume by asking how editorial changes, made both to D&C 42 in particular and to the whole of the Doctrine and Covenants as a collection, shape the meaning and understanding of the revealed law. What draws Spencer's attention in particular is the fact that editorial changes made directly to the text of D&C 42 (in preparation for its canonical publication in 1835) are in tension with editorial decisions made with regard to the whole collection of revelations (beginning in 1876 and continuing into the present). On his account, however, these tensions productively complicate traditional understandings of the distinction between the historical and the canonical, between supposedly pure origins and supposedly impure traditions. Spencer's reading of D&C 42 within the larger canonical history of the Doctrine and Covenants thus concludes with a suggestion that Mormon theology works with a distinct notion of history more often than is supposed.

Obviously, these essays come nowhere close to exhausting the meaning and richness of section 42 of the Doctrine and Covenants. There are more verses in the revelation that these essays collectively ignore than there are verses on which they severally comment. Yet we hope that the philosophical and theological perspectives outlined here, rooted in substantial historical awareness and careful study of the textual tradition, provide a model for how Latter-day Saints might more productively make sense of a revelation like that of the law of consecration. Here we attempt together to consecrate something of our own training, and we can only hope to see that it helps in some way to spur consecrated study among others.

—Jeremiah John and Joseph M. Spencer

Summary Report

Question 1: What is the significance of the historical context and textual history of Doctrine and Covenants 42?

THE HISTORICAL CONTEXT AND THE TEXTUAL HISTORY of Doctrine and Covenants 42 are, in the end, inseparable. The earliest version of the current text was received on February 9, 1831, originally as a set of distinguishable answers to five different questions raised by the elders of the church. The bulk of that earliest revelation (corresponding to today's D&C 42:11–69) was understood to be the law that the Lord had promised would be given to the Saints upon their arrival at "the Ohio" (see D&C 38:32). Within days of the reception of the law, Joseph Smith received another revelation that briefly explained how the church was to determine its application: "I give unto you a commandment, that when ye are assembled together ye shall note with a pen how to act, and for my church to act upon the points of my law and commandments, which I have given: and thus it shall become a law unto you" (Book of Commandments 45:8–9; cf. D&C 43:8–9). The result of this instruction was that, only two weeks after "The Laws of the Church of Christ" had been given (on February 23, 1831), the elders of the church produced what would become the first revision to the text of the Law (see Book of Commandments 47; cf. D&C 42:74–93).

Revisions of the same sort and in the same spirit were made to the originally received text with some frequency between 1831, when it was originally recorded, and 1835, when it received its final form. Revisions were made when leaders of the church learned the difficulties of implementing the law of consecration and stewardship in Missouri, when it was decided that Joseph Smith's revelations should be officially published as the Book of Commandments (as well as in an official church newspaper), when the high priesthood was introduced to the church, when the United Firm (a joint financial venture undertaken by the leaders in both Missouri and Ohio) was formed, when the Saints were driven from their lands in Jackson County, when the priesthood was organized into quorums, and when it was decided to produce a kind of handbook of instructions for the church (in the form of the Doctrine and Covenants).

The heaviest revisions made between 1831 and 1835 are found in what is now Doctrine and Covenants 42:30–39, the passage outlining the law of consecration and stewardship. These revisions were obviously part of an attempt to keep the Law relevant as the church slowly shifted its attention from establishing a communitarian endeavor in Jackson County to establishing a priesthood-governed people organized around the Kirtland Temple. Thus what began as an order into which one entered by deeding all of one's property to the bishop and receiving in return an assigned stewardship (while what remained over in the bishop's possession was dedicated to outfitting the poor and building a gathering place for Israel) was slowly transformed into a general injunction that one help to assist the poor and to build a gathering place by deeding to the bishop only what was "more than [was] necessary for their support" (D&C 42:33). These changes were accompanied by an important—but subtle—de-emphasis on the practical significance of the Law. Although the Law was regarded in 1831 as one of only two organizational documents for the church (the other was today's section 20 of the Doctrine and Covenants, then referred to as the "Articles and Covenants of the Church"), it was positioned in the first edition of the Doctrine and Covenants as section 13, coming not only long after its original companion (today's section 20 was section 2 in 1835, after the revealed "preface"), but also after what today are sections 107, 84, 102, 86, 88, 6, 24, 29, 35, and 38. (This was further confirmed in a way when the Law was—along with the rest of Joseph Smith's revelations—historicized through the chronological reordering of the sections in the Doctrine and Covenants in 1876, the reordering that assigned the Law to its current position as section 42.)

Every change made between 1831 and 1835 to the text of the Law obviously bears significance for theological reflection on the meaning of consecration. Should the final form of the text, due to its canonical status and its long-term stability (unchanged since 1835), be given greater weight than other versions? Should the original wording of the text be granted a certain privileged status, due perhaps to what might be called its "purity"? Is one of the intermediate versions of the text to be preferred—maybe the last revisions produced before the Saints were driven from their lands in Jackson County? Are there points of particular continuity across the several versions of the text that deserve special theological attention? Is there something to be learned from the very process of change and transformation that occurred during the first years of the revelation's circulation? Might it be, perhaps, that there is still reason to ask how the revelation might be further revised in light of historical experience, collaborative discussion, and consultation with the Lord? Might the complications surrounding the canonical text on consecration be a spur to continuing revelation—whether in the privacy of personal application or through the public word of the Lord through a prophet? These are questions that will continue to call for theological reflection.

Question 2: How should Doctrine and Covenants 42 be understood in relation to the rest of the Doctrine and Covenants?

Several revelations contained in the Doctrine and Covenants prepared the way for the reception of what is now section 42. Section 28 features Oliver Cowdery's assignment in September 1830 to leave for Missouri to preach to "the Lamanites" (D&C 28:8). Section 32 contains the commandment to Parley P. Pratt to join Cowdery, which resulted in a remarkably successful stopover in Kirtland, Ohio, where—among many others—Sidney Rigdon joined the fledgling church. After traveling to New York to meet Joseph Smith, as section 35 records, Rigdon became the Prophet's scribe. The result was that Rigdon joined the Prophet in committing the vision of Enoch to writing, in which appears the earliest description of Zion as a city "of one heart and one mind," among whom "there was no poor" (Moses 7:18). When instruction came a few weeks later for the Saints to "assemble together at the Ohio" (D&C 37:3), Joseph Smith and Sidney Rigdon were thus prepared to receive section 38, a revelation riddled with allusions to Enoch's vision, in which they were told to prepare themselves to have "no laws but my laws" (D&C 38:22), receiving the promise that in Ohio the Lord would "give unto you my law" and they would "be endowed with power from on high" (D&C 38:32). As the revelation made clear, the law to be given would help to ensure that "every man [would] esteem his brother as himself" (D&C 38:24) and that the Saints would be "one" (D&C 38:27), in that one would not be "clothed in robes" while another was "clothed in rags" (D&C 38:26). Section 41 then records a further promise, received just after Joseph Smith arrived in Ohio and only days before section 42 would be given, that "by the prayer of your faith ye shall receive my law" (D&C 41:3).

Moreover, as soon as it was received, the Law of section 42 became the focus of many subsequent revelations now contained in the Doctrine and Covenants. Section 43 contains instructions about how the Saints were to "act" on the Law in a way that they would "be sanctified by that which ye have received" (D&C 43:8–9). The Lord gave further, specific instructions in sections 44, 58, 83, and 98 about how to balance the law of the Lord with the laws of the country. Section 51 states, nonetheless, that the Saints had to be "organized according to my laws" or be "cut off" (D&C 51:2), and similar instructions are found in sections 70 and 85. The last of these even prescribes the production of a "book of the law of God" to be kept by the church (D&C 85:5, 7, 11). Sections 72 and 107 appropriately describe themselves as "addition[s] to the law" (see D&C 72:9, 24; 107:59), section 109 uniquely ties the Law revealed in section 42 to the Kirtland Temple, and an explicit reiteration and expansion of the Law can be found in section 119. Section 88 refers to the Law of section 42 as "the law of Christ" (D&C 88:21), and section 105 refers to the same as "the law of the celestial kingdom" (D&C 105:4,

5; cf. 88:22). Other direct references to section 42 as the law of the church can be found in sections 48, 51, 64, 82, 103, 104, and 107. Furthermore, because section 42 contains, in addition to the law it sets forth, instructions regarding teaching by the Spirit, it seems also to be related to sections of the Doctrine and Covenants that clarify the nature of spiritual gifts—in particular sections 46 and 50. Because the officers of the church were to pray for the Spirit but "not teach" if they "receive not the Spirit" (D&C 42:14), further revelation became necessary when some "received ... spirits which ye could not understand, and received them to be of God" (D&C 50:15).

In the first years of the church's establishment, a different sort of relationship existed between section 42 (the "Law of the Church") and what is now section 20 (the "Articles and Covenants of the Church"). This relationship seems to have been established in part by a reference to section 20 in the preamble to the portion of section 42 comprising the Law (see D&C 42:13). Sections 20 and 42 were jointly unique among Joseph Smith's earliest revelations, since they were addressed to and set forth instructions for the entire church, while most other revelations were addressed, patriarchal-blessing-like, to individuals seeking guidance from the Lord. Consequently, sections 20 and 42 were copied and circulated widely among members of the church before they appeared in print, and they were often used in missionary preaching and read in regional conferences held by the Saints. Likewise, these sections appeared, one after the other, on the front pages of the first two issues of the church's first official newspaper, *The Evening and the Morning Star*, in 1832. Their close connection, however, was largely broken by the increased attention given in the church to priesthood organization (section 20 is largely concerned with such organization, while section 42 is not). When the first edition of the Doctrine and Covenants appeared in 1835, despite the fact that the revelations were arranged in order of organizational importance rather than date of original reception, many pages and ten lengthy revelations separated the two from each other.

Today the connection between the two revelations remains, for the most part, broken. Section 20 is still understood as a guide to the structure and organization of the church, while section 42 is largely regarded as a historical artifact whose relevance to the life of faith today is complicated, if not troubled. Nonetheless, given the trajectory of revelations leading up to section 42, as well as the many references back to and clarifications of section 42 in subsequent revelations, those who reflect on the theological significance of the Law should recognize its centrality to the entire project of the Doctrine and Covenants.

Question 3: What is the meaning of "consecration" in Doctrine and Covenants 42?

In this dispensation, consecration was first taught in what is now section 42 of the Doctrine and Covenants and was elaborated on and emphasized in revelations that came after. Most obviously, consecration is at the heart of what is called the Law of the church. It is not a merely temporary project or a commandment given for a particular time and place, but an enduring element of God's will for his people and a necessary dimension of the common life of church members. Church members today do not practice the specific form of "consecration and stewardship" described in section 42, and there is some doubt whether the church ever implemented something similar to this plan on a wide scale. For this reason, any interpretation of the idea of consecration must come to terms with the enduring significance of consecration, bound up as it is with a particular program of economic communalism that is not now and perhaps never was widely implemented. The teaching of consecration in section 42 is the most natural starting place for thinking through this question.

Various forms of the word *consecration* are used six times in Doctrine and Covenants 42:30–39. The original readers of these verses would have understood the common dictionary sense of the term at the time, which is "to set apart, dedicate, or devote to the service and worship of God" (*Webster's 1828 Dictionary*). In the original revelation, the Lord tells the Saints to "consecrate all thy properties ... unto me" (Book of Commandments 44:26). But beyond this command, the revelation teaches that the proper way to dedicate properties to God is to remember the poor by contributing to a system that ensures their support. Consecration is also inseparable from stewardship, that is, providing diligently for our own support and for a surplus to be given

to the bishop for building the kingdom of God. What Doctrine and Covenants 42 reveals about consecration is that dedicating ourselves and our property to God means giving it up for the support of the poor and using it ourselves for the purposes of God's kingdom.

Revisions of the text between the 1831 revelation and the published text of 1835 make the demands of the Law somewhat less specific and increase emphasis on concern for the poor. A revision to verse 39 also makes clear what was already contained in the original revelation: that consecration is a willing commitment to God's church and its poor, not a forcible dedication or despoiling of nonbelievers to believers. In the wake of the historical and textual changes made to the revelation that now comprises Doctrine and Covenants 42, the meaning and connotations of the term *consecration* have shifted. For example, in the original 1831 revelation, only one act of consecration was called for, and it required consecration of "all thy properties" (Book of Commandments 44:26). For the 1835 edition, the word *all* had been changed to *of* (D&C 42:30). Moreover, in the 1835 edition, Doctrine and Covenants 42:33 refers to a "first consecration," suggesting that the act of consecrating "of thy properties" should be understood as only the first step of a larger, more demanding law.

This shift from a unilateral to a more partitioned conception of consecration has implications for church members' responsibilities. In particular, the 1831 text mentions only a mediated responsibility between church members and "the poor and needy" (Book of Commandments 44:29; cf. D&C 42:34), whereas the 1835 text calls for more direct concern for the poor. This shift is implemented in the 1835 text by inserting the word *poor* four times (once each in verses 30, 31, 37, and 39 of D&C 42). This shift is also reflected in the textual change from God's original call for a consecration of properties "unto me" (Book of Commandments 44:26) to a later call for consecration of properties "unto them," meaning the poor (D&C 42:30). With the 1831 text, consecration entailed giving one's properties to God and then letting the church care for the poor. However, with the 1835 text, church members came to share more directly in this responsibility for the poor.

In a certain sense, the insertions of *the poor* into the text could be seen as increasing the responsibilities imposed on church members.

As a practical matter, however, these textual changes coincided with a shift away from the original immediacy in the call to live the law of consecration. Church members to this day covenant to live the law of consecration, but this covenantal form of consecration has been uncoupled from the church-wide practice described in the Book of Commandments. This uncoupling might be understood as a reflection of a more general assimilationist tendency in Mormonism in which boundaries and tensions between Mormons and their neighbors have become more porous and less pronounced. This assimilationist trajectory can be traced back to an earlier section of the Law, D&C 42:18–29, where the commandments quoted from the Decalogue are taken only from the second tablet and contain ethical injunctions upheld by a wide range of non-Mormon religions and humanitarians.

If communal boundaries thus play an important role in how we understand Mormonism's historically constituted understanding of consecration, then the textual changes pertaining to the relation of Israelites and gentiles have particular theological import. Originally, Book of Commandments 44:32 read, "For I will consecrate the riches of the Gentiles, unto my people which are of the house of Israel." This text has resonance with Isaiah 61:6, which describes a day when the Israelites would "eat the riches of the Gentiles," and was interpreted by some early Mormons in a way that fueled tensions between Latter-day Saints and their neighbors. This text was changed and expanded to the following in the 1835 edition of the Law (additions and changes are italicized): "for I will consecrate *of* the riches of *those who embrace my gospel among* the Gentiles unto *the poor of* my people *who* are of the house of Israel" (D&C 42:39). These textual changes describe a very different relationship between gentiles and Mormons/Israelites. On the one hand, these changes presage the eventual overcoming of cultural tensions between Mormons and their neighbors, a trajectory that culminated in the relative embrace of Mormons in the mid-twentieth century. On the other hand, these changes are a deferral of the original radical vision and call for a community of fully consecrated members living with "no poor among them" (Moses 7:18).

Question 4: In what sense does section 42 embrace the law of the church? What is meant by law here? How is the giving of the law in section 42 related to the project of gathering and the establishment of the New Jerusalem?

In the fall of 1830, just a few months after the establishment of the church, the restoration of the gospel began to take on a political significance. Missionaries were called to preach in Missouri, and Joseph Smith told the Saints that the location of the "city Zion"—the biblical New Jerusalem—would soon be revealed (D&C 28:9). That same fall, in the revelation that is now Doctrine and Covenants 29, the Lord called the leaders of the church "to bring to pass the gathering of mine elect … that they shall be gathered in unto one place" (D&C 29:7, 8). A few weeks later, the church was commanded to assemble in Ohio (D&C 37:3), and in January of 1831, the Lord told the church through revelation that "there I will give unto you my law; and there you shall be endowed with power from on high" (D&C 38:32).

This law was revealed the following month and would become section 42 of the Doctrine and Covenants. The revelations had contained "commandments" and even "church articles" and "covenants" before this time, so "the law" was something different. The first difference in the Law of section 42 was that it was explicitly connected with the task of gathering and building up the city Zion in preparation for the second coming of Christ. The second difference was that this new law (or newly revealed law) was to be something like a constitution for God's people, or a framework for a way of life God's people were commanded to live. "Church articles" (like those found in section 20) were much more like a set of bylaws, together with a discussion of the atonement of Christ and the restoration of the gospel. The Law, on the other hand, gives a discussion of legal rules, loosely based on parts of the Decalogue, together with consecration and stewardship, but proceeds to describe the character of gathered Zion and lays out the blessings that will come to God's people as they are "gathered in one" and live God's law. Like Deuteronomy, the Law would give prescriptions and prohibitions (including several that were given again, specifically in verses

18–29, which resemble parts of the Decalogue), along with promised blessings for obedience and punishments for disobedience. Finally, the Law was a different kind of revealed commandment in that it made suggestions toward the political and economic independence of God's people. Initially the Law seemed to establish a system of justice and an economic community that was independent from the world. In this way, the Law was the fulfillment of Doctrine and Covenants 38, in which the Lord said that "in time ye shall have no king nor ruler, for I will be your king and watch over you.... You shall be a free people, and ye shall have no laws but my laws when I come, for I am your lawgiver, and what can stay my hand?" (vv. 21–22).

These suggestions of political sovereignty were softened later. For example, after first prescribing the punishment of murderers, the Law was revised to turn them over to the law of the land. More important, perhaps, the commandments regarding consecration and steward-ship were revised too, in part to place properties held as stewardships on stronger legal footing in American courts. The ease with which these revisions took place is itself notable. The Lord had declared that the Saints would have "no laws but my laws when I come," but in the meantime the sovereignty of God's kingdom could not yet be realized. After all, the Law was a preparatory law, and the specifics of these preparatory arrangements could be adapted to the temporal realities of the church.

Doctrine and Covenants 42 was given in response to five questions asked by Joseph Smith and others at Kirtland, Ohio, in February 1831. Two of the questions directly concern gathering: "Shall the Church come together into one place or remain as they are in separate bodies?" and "[What is] the Law regulating the Church in her present situation till the time of her gathering?"

The first question should be interpreted as having an immediate, short-term significance. By the time of the Prophet's arrival in Ohio, it had already been revealed that the Saints would "be gathered in unto one place upon the face of the land" (D&C 29:8) and that the "city Zion" would be built "on the borders by the Lamanites" (D&C 28:9). The question of the elders that prompted the revelation of section 42, then, was about the timing of the promised gathering. In answer to that question, verses 8–9 instruct the elders to build up the church "in every region ... until the time shall come when it shall be revealed ... when the city of the New Jerusalem shall be prepared." In verses 35–36, the Lord makes clear that consecration is for the purpose of "building up ... the New Jerusalem ... that my covenant people may be gathered in one in that day when I shall come to my temple." But out of necessity, consecration was only attempted in those places where the Saints were most concentrated in one area. Consecration and stewardship was first attempted in Kirtland and then later in Missouri.

An important change to the text between 1831 and 1835 that is relevant to the work of gathering is an increased concern for the poor in the discussion of consecration. While the 1831 text asks the Saints to consecrate their goods to God and explains that these donations will then be used to establish stewardships to care for the "poor and needy" (Book of Commandments 44:29; cf. D&C 42:34), the 1835 text calls for more direct concern for the poor. The 1835 text begins the discussion of consecration with the statement "thou wilt remember the poor" and inserts the word *poor* three additional times (once each in verses 31, 37 and 39 of D&C 42). In the original text the Lord calls Saints to consecrate properties "unto me" (Book of Commandments 44:26), but the same passage in the 1835 text has the Lord speaking of imparting properties "unto them," meaning the poor (D&C 42:30). Some historical context explains the shift in emphasis. The systems of consecration and stewardships are said to be established with a "covenant and a deed" that cannot be broken, but the legal form these arrangements took were unusual in the context of American law. Specifically, non-Mormon courts took a dim view of the church's claim upon the "stewardships" of former church members and almost always decided against the church's claims.

On the other hand, emphasizing that consecration was the way to "remember the poor" was not merely a legal maneuver. The most urgent work of gathering in Kirtland and in Missouri was very often the task of providing for newly arrived members, who were often without means for their support. This was equally true in Nauvoo and later Utah, where building up the church meant providing livelihoods for "the poor of my people" (D&C 42:39).

"I Will Give unto You My Law": Section 42 as a Legal Text and the Paradoxes of Divine Law

Nathan B. Oman

DIVINE LAW OCCUPIES AN UNEASY PLACE in the modern world, thanks to a long history. For thinkers in antiquity, divine law was hypothetical.[1] They did not identify it with the actual rules that operated within a particular society. One might sanctify one's traditions, but neither Solon nor Lycurgus was a Moses delivering a legal code claiming divine authorship. In the Middle Ages, however, Muslims, Jews, and Christians sought to turn divine law into a juridical reality. Indeed, what we today call a "religion" was then referred to as a "law." Hence, medievals spoke of the law of Christ, the law of the Jews, or the law of the Saracens rather than of Christianity, Judaism, or Islam. The concrete effort to realize divine law created conflicting jurisdictional claims that resulted in clashes between secular and religious authority such as the murder of Thomas Becket, Archbishop of Canterbury, by knights of Henry II of England in 1170.

---

1. See generally Rémi Brague, *The Law of God: The Philosophical History of an Idea* (Chicago: University of Chicago Press, 2008).

These clashes had their origin in the disintegration of the primal legal unity represented by the idea of divine law.[2] Early canonists at the outset of the medieval era cast the church as an integrated legal system. Later, royal chanceries set up their own legal systems in imitation of the church, which made possible conflicts such as that between Henry II and his "troublesome priest." Still later, as power consolidated in national governments, the relationship between divine and secular law gradually reversed. Law ceased to be primarily a matter of scriptural exegesis and increasingly became something like the common law of England: a set of rules promulgated by a secular political authority. In the contemporary world, we arrive at the Weberian ideal of law as the rationalization of the state's monopoly on legitimate violence. And in such a context, divine law has few places it can take root—other than in the realm of the private, the moral, or the religious.

Section 42 of the Doctrine and Covenants (D&C) represents a Mormon response to the predicament of divine law in modernity. The text, originally presented as "The Laws of the Church of Christ," is a jurisprudential document, one that purports to come from God. It thus presents itself as divine law. A careful reading of the text, however, shows the way in which the idea of divine law at work in section 42 is defined in part through a dialogue with the secular law. Several historians have argued that early Mormons adopted a "theocratic ethic" in which the prophetic commands of revelation were held superior to any demand of secular law.[3] But whatever the merits of this view as a historical interpretation of the ideology of nineteenth-century Mormonism, the text of section 42 reveals a more ambiguous position.[4] On one hand, the text seems to challenge the sovereignty of the

---

2. See generally Harold Berman, *Law and Revolution: The Formation of Western Legal Tradition* (Cambridge, MA: Harvard University Press, 1983).

3. D. Michael Quinn is the author of this interpretation, which has been followed by several other scholars. See Quinn, *The Mormon Hierarchy: Origins of Power* (Salt Lake City: Signature Books, 1994); see also Gary James Bergera, *Conflict in the Quorum: Orson Pratt, Brigham Young, Joseph Smith* (Salt Lake City: Signature Books, 2002).

4. This is not a challenge per se to the interpretation that Quinn and Bergera offer of a particular period in Mormon history. I believe that at times their claims are overstated, but this is a distinct issue from the exegesis of section 42, which is my sole concern in this essay.

state. At the same time, it both retreats from such challenges and molds itself in dialogue with the secular law's treatment of the practices it defines. For its part, the idea of a theocratic ethic presents a relatively simple model of the relationship between divine and human law, in which the demands of the revealed law are always held to be superior to and sovereign over the demands of secular law. But this model does not adequately capture the idea of divine law revealed in section 42. Rather, the revelation provides a way of accommodating divine law to the reality of secular dominance. The approach first seen in section 42 was dramatically repeated in Mormonism's abandonment of polygamy at the end of the nineteenth century.

In this essay, I explore the idea of divine law that emerges from section 42. First, I show how the revelation operates as a legal text. Such an interpretation makes the best sense of its textual history. I then argue that what the text offers to readers is ultimately a paradox, a divine law that ignores competing sovereignties in its assertion of authority while simultaneously sacralizing its own accommodation to modern legal realities. While lacking the simplicity of a theocratic ethic, this approach allows divine law to continue operating in a world where secular legal regimes claim overwhelming practical dominance.

Exegesis of section 42 begins with its textual history. On January 2, 1831, Joseph Smith received a revelation now canonized as section 38. Some months earlier, Mormon missionaries on their way to Missouri to preach to the Lamanites had converted a large group of Campbellites and Baptist primitivists in Kirtland, Ohio. At the time, Joseph Smith was still living in New York. The January revelation commanded that the Saints "should go to the Ohio" (D&C 38:32). It went on to promise, in God's voice, that "there I will give unto you my law" (D&C 38:32). Accordingly, Joseph relocated his family to Kirtland the next month, and beginning on February 9 began receiving the promised law.[5] What would eventually become section 42 was received in three parts on two separate days. The initial version of what was to become Doctrine

---

5. For an account of Joseph Smith's move to Kirtland and the circumstances in which what became section 42 was given, see Richard Lyman Bushman, *Joseph Smith, Rough Stone Rolling* (New York: Alfred A. Knopf, 2005), 122–26, 144–55.

and Covenants 42:1–69 was first recorded on February 9, 1831.[6] The first part of this text dealt with various missionary callings (see D&C 42:1–10), while the core of what came to be called "the Law" lies behind what is now D&C 42:11–69. Subsequently, on February 23 Joseph met with a group to consider "how the Elders of the church of Christ are to act upon the points of the Law" and recorded the initial version of what eventually became D&C 42:70–93, which provided a gloss on the previously received text.[7] Further, as will be discussed below, the Law was substantially revised before settling into its current form, but from the beginning it was self-consciously presented as "the law which I [the Lord] shall give unto you" (D&C 42:2)—that is, as a legal text. (When John Whitmer transcribed Joseph's revelations into an official notebook kept in Kirtland and later in Missouri, he generally prefaced each new entry with the word "Commandment," written in large letters.[8] However, when he recorded the text of what would become D&C 42:1–72, he wrote in large script "The Laws of the Church of Christ.")[9]

It might be surprising that the text of the revelation was altered. But legal texts are practical documents. Their purpose is to give guidance in particular contexts by providing rules. The idea that the text changes to reflect new rules and practices is unobjectionable.[10] Indeed, we expect this of legal texts. And the complex textual history of section 42 suggests that it originally functioned in part as a legal text in this

---

6. Grant Underwood, "'The Laws of the Church of Christ' (D&C 42): A Textual and Historical Analysis," in *The Doctrine and Covenants: Revelations in Context*, ed. Andrew H. Hedges, J. Spencer Fluhman, and Alonzo L. Gaskill (Provo, UT: BYU Religious Studies Center and Deseret Book, 2008), 109.

7. See Underwood, "'Laws of the Church of Christ,'" 111–12.

8. See Robin Scott Jensen, Robert J. Woodford, and Steven C. Harper, eds., *Manuscript Revelation Books*, facsimile edition, first volume of the Revelations and Translations series of *The Joseph Smith Papers*, ed. Dean C. Jessee, Ronald K. Esplin, and Richard Lyman Bushman (Salt Lake City: Church Historian's Press, 2009), 86, 92, 104.

9. See Jensen, Woodford, and Harper, *Manuscript Revelation Books*, 94.

10. Or at least mostly unobjectionable. Lon Fuller famously argued that a law that shifted too rapidly threatened the concept of the rule of law, what Fuller called "the internal morality of law." See generally Fuller, *The Morality of Law*, rev. ed. (New Haven: Yale University Press, 1969).

way.[11] The earliest manuscript of section 42 no longer exists, but we do have numerous prepublication copies made by individual Latter-day Saints, as well as more official compilations kept by Joseph Smith's scribes. Additionally, various versions of the texts that eventually became section 42 were published in *The Evening and the Morning Star*, the 1833 Book of Commandments, and the first edition of the Doctrine and Covenants in 1835. These early versions of section 42 show that the original text was substantially revised prior to its 1835 canonical presentation. The legal character of the text suggests how Latter-day Saints negotiated these changes. According to Orson Pratt, Joseph Smith distinguished between revelations that were published as authorities to the community and revelations that were merely of historical significance—a distinction that suggests a quasi-legal understanding of the revelation's textuality.[12]

Likewise, the minutes of the Kirtland High Council in 1834, where the decision was made to compile what became the 1835 edition of the Doctrine and Covenants, suggest a similarly ahistorical, legalistic understanding of the text. "The Council then proceeded to appoint a committee to arrange the items of the doctrine of Jesus Christ, for the government of the Church of Latter-Day Saints.... These items are to be taken from the Bible, Book of Mormon, and the revelations which have been given to the Church up to this date, or shall be until such

---

11. For a detailed discussion of that textual history, see generally Underwood, "'Laws of the Church of Christ'"; Robert J. Woodford, "The Historical Development of the Doctrine and Covenants" (PhD diss., Brigham Young University, 1974), 525–69. For Joseph Smith's manuscript copies of the revelations that became section 42, see Jensen, Woodford, and Harper, *Manuscript Revelation Books*, 95–105, 107.

12. Orson Pratt wrote, "Joseph, the Prophet, in selecting the revelations from the Manuscripts, and arranging them for publication, did not arrange them according to the order of the date in which they were given, neither did he think it necessary to publish them all in the Book of Doctrine and Covenants, but left them to be published more fully in his History. Hence, paragraphs taken from the revelations of a later date, are, in a few instances, incorporated with those of an earlier date. Indeed, at the time of compilation, the Prophet was inspired in several instances to write additional sentences and paragraphs to the earlier revelations." *Millennial Star* 17 (25 April 1857): 260.

arrangements are made."[13] Notice that the Doctrine and Covenants is compiled "for the government of the Church." Envisioning something quite distinct from a mere record of past revelations, the council contemplated a compilation of scriptures from multiple sources that would then serve as an authoritative guide to current practice.[14]

Consider some passages in what appears today as verses 30–37 of section 42. These verses set forth rules governing the consecration of property to the church and the deeding back to members of individual stewardships. The procedures described in the earliest manuscript copy of the Law are different from those found in the final version. In Joseph Smith's manuscript notebook, for example, the text describes the procedure for administering any residual property remaining in the hands of the church after stewardships have been doled out to members. It reads, "The Residue shall be kept in my Store house to administer to the poor & needy as shall be appointed by the Elders of the Church & the Bishop."[15] This version of the text was then included in the 1833 Book of Commandments.[16] In the 1835 edition of the Doctrine and Covenants, however, the decision-making body controlling the residue of property was designated as "the high council of the church, and the

---

13. "Minutes of the High Council, Kirtland, September 24, 1834," *Millennial Star* 15 (March 19, 1853): 183.

14. It is interesting to compare the structure contemplated by the Kirtland High Council's resolution with the earliest governing document for the church, the "Articles of the Church of Christ," written in 1829. The Articles were drawn up by Oliver Cowdery in 1829 and were almost immediately replaced by what became section 20 of the Doctrine and Covenants. The Articles are written in the first person by the voice of the Lord, but the substance consists largely of verbatim quotations from the ecclesiological passages in the Book of Mormon, particularly in Moroni, strongly suggesting that Oliver Cowdery simply compiled scriptural passages to create a governing document for the then-contemplated church. See generally Scott H. Faulring, "An Examination of the 1829 'Articles of the Church of Christ' in Relation to Section 20 of the Doctrine and Covenants," *BYU Studies* 43/4 (2004): 57–91.

15. Jensen, Woodford, and Harper, *Manuscript Revelation Books*, 99.

16. Robin Scott Jensen, Richard E. Turley Jr., and Riley M. Lorimer, eds., *Revelations and Translations, Volume 2: Published Revelations*, vol. 2 of the Revelations and Translations series of *The Joseph Smith Papers*, edited by Dean C. Jessee, Ronald K. Esplin, and Richard Lyman Bushman (Salt Lake City: Church Historian's Press, 2011), 104.

bishop and his council," reflecting the more elaborate ecclesiastical structure that had been created in the intervening years.[17] Likewise, the earliest version of the text seems to contemplate a single act of consecration upon conversion.[18] In contrast, the 1835 edition introduces a second consecration "if there shall be properties in the hands of the church, or any individuals of it, more than is necessary for their support" (see D&C 43:33).[19] As Grant Underwood points out, all these changes passed without comment at the time, suggesting that early Mormons understood the evolution of the text not as the corruption of a divine original but simply as a juridical updating.[20] Just as the US Code is only accidentally a record of particular legislative enactments, serving primarily and essentially as a compendium of currently valid law, the text of the 1835 Doctrine and Covenants was less a record of a distinct revelatory event than the product of successive "legislative" amendments. All these exegetical details suggest that the Law of section 42 is to be understood as a law in more than one sense.

Of course, law is a famously slippery concept. All the words common in Western thought that could be rendered as "law"—*nomos, lex, ius, aequitas, Recht, loi, droit*, right, equity, and so forth—have slightly different meanings. Lon Fuller's broad definition of law as the process of subjecting human action to the government of rules, however, is capacious enough for us to refer to section 42 as law without embarrassment.[21] And we have already seen some clear reasons to believe that the revelation should be regarded as a legal text. Still, we can ask in exactly what sense the Laws of the Church of Christ is law. Understanding a legal text as the product of successive rounds of legislative

---

17. Jensen, Turley, and Lorimer, *Published Revelations*, 432. The current edition of the Doctrine and Covenants follows the 1835 version of the text of D&C 42.

18. See Jensen, Woodford, and Harper, *Manuscript Revelation Books*, 99–100.

19. Compare Jensen, Turley, and Lorimer, *Published Revelations*, 99, setting forth the original procedure.

20. See Underwood, "'Laws of the Church of Christ,'" 114.

21. See, e.g., Lon L. Fuller, "Law as an Instrument of Social Control and Law as a Facilitation of Human Interaction," *Brigham Young University Law Review* 1975/1 (1975): 95. "Rules can emerge and become effective as law without receiving the imprimatur of any explicitly legislative organ of government."

amendment provides a way of understanding the revision of the Laws of the Church of Christ between 1831 and 1835. For all of that evolution, however, section 42 also aligns itself with a more cosmic vision of *divine* law.

Legislation was an idea familiar in the America of the 1830s,[22] but there is another way of thinking about law that is profoundly uncomfortable with the idea of legal change. This approach presents a continuum. At one end is the notion of law as an ancient and sanctified (but nonetheless conventional) tradition, as in the Roman *mos maiorum*.[23] At the other end is the notion of law as a timeless statement of cosmic truth. For example, during the classical period, Muslim theologians argued that the Qur'an—and with it the *sharia*—was an uncreated emanation from God.[24] Section 42 invokes something of this more eternal notion of law, although where it falls between the *mos maiorum* and the uncreated Qur'an is unclear. As noted earlier, the Laws of the Church of Christ proper does not begin until verse 11 in the current edition of the Doctrine and Covenants, verses 1–10 being concerned with individual missionary callings. In verses 18–29, which form a kind of preface to the rapidly evolving material on the law of consecration, the Law recapitulates in effect the second half of the Decalogue (the latter six of the Ten Commandments). It thus simultaneously links itself to the ancient order of things going back to the

---

22. For a discussion of the role of legislation during the early nineteenth century, see Kermit Hall, *The Magic Mirror: Law in American History* (New York: Oxford University Press, 1989), 87–105.

23. Ancient Roman jurists thought of law in terms of the *mos maiorum*, the ancient traditions of the city dating back to the Laws of the Twelve Tables. On this view, legislation was seen as suspect innovation at best. At worse, it was—literally, given the religious significance of the *mos maiorum*—a form of sacrilege. See Hans Wolff, *Roman Law: An Historical Introduction* (Norman: University of Oklahoma Press, 1978), 63. Of course, the Romans maintained a distinction between secular law, *ius*, and sacral law, *fas*, but this did not mean that *ius* was bereft of religious significance, just that it didn't necessarily govern cultic practices, which were left to priests and augers.

24. According to these theologians the Qur'an "endures forever with and through the divine Ipseity and is indivisible from it, with neither beginning nor end in eternity." Henry Corbin, *History of Islamic Philosophy*, trans. Phillip Sherrard (London: Kegan Paul International, 1993), 11.

children of Israel and invokes what nineteenth-century Americans—influenced as they were by Protestant thought—saw as a changeless standard of God's moral truth. By recapitulating the scriptural prohibitions against theft, murder, and adultery, the revelation was thus laying claim to being something more than a compendium of current policies regarding consecrated properties.

Moderns, of course, identify law with rules promulgated by the state.[25] Max Weber, as already noted, captured the common sense of modernity when he defined the state as "the form of human community that (successfully) lays claim to the monopoly of legitimate physical violence."[26] Modernity's common sense couples this view with the positivist position that there is a conceptually sharp distinction between law and morals, mere counsel and threats backed by legitimate violence. Tellingly, Grant Underwood discusses section 42's recapitulation of part of the Decalogue as "the Church's moral code" and the "ethical vision of the Ten Commandments."[27] By invoking concepts—moral and ethical—that modern positivism conceptually separates from the legal, Underwood here imposes on the text a set of categories that the text itself does not embrace. On this point, it is striking that the Law explicitly challenges the state's Weberian monopoly on force, declaring, "thou shalt not kill. he that k[i]lleth shall die" (see D&C 42:19).[28]

The way in which section 42 recapitulates the Decalogue underlines its legal and political function. The connection between section 42 and Exodus runs deep. The story of Sinai in Exodus 20, one of the two places in the Bible where the Ten Commandments are given, marks a key moment in the narrative of God's chosen people. The children of Israel have been slaves in Egypt, living under the yoke of Pharaoh. Having escaped his armies through the miraculous parting of the Red

---

25. This idea was just beginning to receive a forcefully philosophical articulation at the time Joseph Smith began publishing his revelations. See John Austin, *The Province of Jurisprudence Determined* and *The Uses of the Study of Jurisprudence* (Indianapolis: Hackett, 1998).

26. Max Weber, *The Vocation Lectures*, ed. David Owen and Tracy B. Strong, trans. Rodney Livingstone (Indianapolis: Hackett, 2004), 33.

27. Underwood, "'Laws of the Church of Christ,'" 117.

28. Jensen, Woodford, and Harper, *Manuscript Revelation Books*, 99.

Sea, they find themselves for the first time beyond the political sover-eignty of Egypt. And it is at *this* moment that God delivers to Moses his law. It is the transmission of the law from God to Moses and from Moses to the people that founds them as a political community. Prior to Exodus 20, the children of Israel are slaves or fugitives, the opposite of an autonomous polity; after the promulgation of God's law at Sinai, they are no longer merely a household—or worse, slaves, adjuncts to the household of Pharaoh—but instead they become a nation. In the language of classical political philosophy, the Decalogue marks the transformation of the people from an *oikos* to a distinct *polis* with its own *nomos*.

All this is strikingly reflected in the historical context of section 42's original reception. In the January 1831 revelation mentioned at the outset of this essay, the Lord vouchsafed the Saints "a land of promise, a land flowing with milk and honey" (D&C 38:18). The revelation went on to link this promised land with the foundation of a new and sover-eign community: "But, verily I say unto you that in time ye shall have no king nor ruler, for I will be your king and watch over you. Where-fore, hear my voice and follow me, and you shall be a free people, and ye shall have no laws but my laws when I come, for I am your lawgiver, and what can stay my hand?" (D&C 38:21–22). The revelation then commands Joseph to "go to the Ohio," but Kirtland is not the promised land. That is to be located in Jackson County, Missouri. Rather, Ohio is a stopping place where, the Lord promises, "I will give unto you my law" (D&C 38:32). Joseph's revelations thus explicitly place the coming forth of the Laws of the Church of Christ in the narrative context of the exodus, with Kirtland as a new Mount Sinai, whence issues a new law that founds a new community set to inherit a new promised land.[29]

The New Testament, however, complicates this reading of section 42. The synoptic Gospels use the same narrative motif to mark the foundation of the Christian community but in a context that never makes of the Decalogue a replacement of rival earthly authorities. In

---

29. I am indebted to Joseph Spencer for pointing out to me the way in which sec-tion 38 reinforces the nesting of the Laws of the Church of Christ in the Sinai narrative in Exodus.

the Sermon on the Mount, Jesus, acting as a new Moses, delivers to his followers a new law on the mountaintop, and it is this new law that then founds them as a community. Indeed, in the famous hypertheses of the sermon—"Ye have heard it said ... But I say unto you ..." (see Matthew 5:21–45)—Jesus recapitulates key portions of the law given to Moses at Sinai. But even as he is presented as the lawgiver, the same Jesus of the synoptic Gospels emphatically declares his willingness to render unto Caesar the things that are Caesar's (see Matthew 22:21), just as Paul was anxious to make clear that Christians should submit themselves to "the powers that be" (see Romans 13:1). We thus have two distinct models for the founding of a community via the Decalogue: the unlimited sovereignty of Israel in the Hebrew scriptures, but also the nonstatist claims of New Testament Christianity. Strikingly, the Zion founded by the partial recapitulation of the Decalogue in section 42 takes an ambivalent, middle position between these two poles.

The tendency toward one of these poles can be witnessed before the revelation that would become section 42 was given. The January 1831 revelation mentioned before (now D&C 38) speaks of the law in relationship to political sovereignty—"ye shall have no king nor ruler" and "ye shall have no laws but my laws when I come" (vv. 21, 22)—suggesting the primacy of the Sinai narrative rather than the Sermon on the Mount. This tendency then appears also in section 42. In fact, at least two textual features of the Laws of the Church of Christ point toward the more aggressive position represented by the nation of Israel. First, recall that verses 70–93 in the current version of section 42 were not part of the original law. Rather they were added subsequently to instruct "how the Elders of the church of Christ are to act upon the points of the Law."[30] This is important because these verses disclaim the death penalty announced in the original text of the Laws of the Church of Christ (again: "He that k[i]lleth shall die"). Instead, the later addition commands that criminal malefactors are to be "delivered up and dealt with according to the laws of the land; ... and it shall be proved according to the laws of the land" (D&C 42:79). But this clarification—a gloss that provides an alternative procedure for dealing with the reality of a

---

30. Underwood, "'Laws of the Church of Christ,'" 111–12.

functioning secular law—throws into relief the original law's insistence upon the death penalty for murderers. Tellingly, the initial prohibition is not treated as a justification for the secular legal regime; rather it is treated as an alternative to it.

The second aspect of the revelation that takes a more aggressive stance on sovereignty lies in the specific way the original Laws of the Church of Christ recapitulates the Decalogue. According to one tradition, the commandments contained in the first half of the Decalogue—the prohibitions on polytheism, idolatry, and the like—all relate to matters governing humanity's relationship with God. In contrast, the commandments contained in the so-called second tablet—the commands against coveting, theft, murder, adultery, and so on—all relate to relations between people rather than between people and God.[31] This division tracks a number of fault lines that run deep through Western political thought: the first tablet deals with matters of religion, the second with matters of politics; the first tablet deals with sacred matters, the second with profane; the first tablet deals with matters of church, the second with matters of state. This division has even been mapped epistemologically, with the first tablet identifying wrongs known by special revelation, the second identifying wrongs that can be divined by universal natural reason. If one approaches the Laws of the Church of Christ with this traditional understanding of the Decalogue in mind, it is immediately striking that its recapitulation of the Ten Commandments contains no references to the first tablet and names only commandments from the second tablet. The founding law of Zion plants itself firmly on the political, secular, state, and universal side of the Decalogue. This is, again, suggestive of a certain conflict between revealed law and secular law.

There are, however, features of the current text of section 42 that significantly qualify the way in which the Laws of the Church of Christ challenges the sovereignty of the secular law. First, as just noted again,

---

31. See, e.g., John Calvin, *Institutes of the Christian Religion*, ed. John T. McNeill, trans. Ford Lewis Battles (Philadelphia: Westminster John Knox Press, 1960), 376–77. "God has so divided his law into two parts, which contain the whole of righteousness, as to assigning the first part to those duties of religion which particularly concern the worship of his majesty; the second to the duties of law that have to do with men."

verses 70–93 of the current text were given separately from the original law. They came in response to a very concrete, practical question from the elders assembled in Kirtland. Having been given the law, they wanted to know what to do in concrete practice. Strikingly, this further revelation (received only two weeks after the original) retreats from the more absolute claims made in the original law of February 9. Most dramatically, as already noted, the call for the death penalty is relaxed, with malefactors being given over to the ordinarily constituted legal authorities. Likewise, the implementing verses in this section assume an ecclesiastical jurisdiction independent of the state to try matters such as adultery but with its remedial options clearly limited to excommunication from the ecclesiastical community.

Further, as discussed earlier, later editorial alterations to the text of the original law—especially in connection with procedures involving the consecrations of properties—put on display a revealed law that is in dialogue with the secular legal system. In particular, two changes in the text minimize the confrontation between the law of consecration and stewardship and the common law rules of property. First, after the text has been edited, there is no longer any attempt by the church to retain a property interest in the stewardships. The earlier regime had assumed that even after property was given as part of a stewardship the bishop would retain the discretion to alter the allotment. Allowing such fractured control over property, however, was anathema to the common law of nineteenth-century America. It smacked of the repudiated doctrine of feudal tenures and seemed inconsistent with the allodial character of American real property.[32] Unsurprisingly, the result of the original law's organization of affairs was litigation against the church by disaffected members—litigation that generally did not go in the church's favor.[33] Hence, the text was altered so that property was

---

32. For a detailed discussion of how the law of consecration and stewardship clashed with the ideology of common law property rules in the United States, see Nathan B. Oman, "'The Living Oracles': Legal Interpretation and Mormon Thought," *Dialogue: A Journal of Mormon Thought* 42/2 (2009): 1.

33. See Edwin Brown Firmage and Richard Collin Mangrum, *Zion in the Courts: A Legal History of the Church of Jesus Christ of Latter-day Saints, 1830–1900* (Chicago: University of Illinois Press, 1988), 62.

given "with a covenant and a deed [note the inclusion of the technical, legal term] which cannot be broken" (D&C 42:30). This change in the text marks a retreat from ecclesiastical control over property once it had been given as part of a stewardship. Prior to the change, the church claimed the right to repossess property given as part of a stewardship; after the change, the recipient of such property owned it free and clear of any ecclesiastical claims.

The fully revised version of the law also emphasizes in various places the fact that consecrations to the church were for the care of the poor and benefit of church officers. One of the legal problems with the system of consecration and stewardship was that the deeding of property to the church followed by an immediate deed from the church back to the individual—the procedure generally employed in consecrations—looked like a dummy transaction of the kind the common law has always treated suspiciously.[34] On the other hand, gifts to eleemosynary institutions or for the support of ministers are examples of transactions that the common law has traditionally been enthusiastic about protecting from subsequent legal attack. Hence, the revised text describing the law of consecration and stewardship did so in terms that were more likely to be treated favorably in litigation. This example, combined with those just discussed, suggests that what is now section 42 is as comfortable within an amiable relationship to secular law as it is with a stronger rivalry with secular law. The revelation draws on both the Sinai narrative's sense of the sovereignty of divine law and the gospel's willingness to work within the context of other laws held to be sovereign.

What are we to make of this complex document? In a sense, the textual history of section 42 recapitulates the history of the idea of divine law, moving from the idea that divine law is a juridical reality to the idea of a divine law that exists in the spaces left open by secular law. That history is compressed from the fourteen centuries beginning with the disintegration of the Roman Empire to the fourteen days between

---

34. Dummy sales, for example, are a classic way of secreting property from creditors. Likewise, immediate sale and deed-back transactions were frequently used as a device for creating security arrangements that were otherwise deemed fraudulent by the early common law.

February 9 and February 23, 1831. The law of February 9 speaks in an imagined space where no competing sovereignty exists, where Zion can be founded in an empty world through a new law delivered by a new Moses. The Saints have no king nor any law but the law of God (see, again, D&C 38:21–22). By February 23, however, the elders require a gloss, instructions on "how [they] ... are to act upon the points of the Law." They find themselves living in a world inhabited by a robust secular law, so they need to know how the divine law is to interact with it. The response then and thereafter is a ceding of murder and the protection of property to the law of the land, coupled with the creation of an ecclesiastical structure to deal with moral questions. In effect, the gloss of February 23 transforms Zion from a kingdom into a church and the divine law into a system of morality.

I want to note two things about this process. First, there is a stunning and daring anachronism in the law of February 9. The problematic relationship of divine and secular law had been a matter of dispute since at least the twelfth century, and early nineteenth-century America offered a perfectly workable solution to this problem in the Protestant settlement between church and state. That solution can be found reflected in the church's statement on government, authored by Oliver Cowdery and canonized as section 134. It comfortably adopts the settlement worked out in the late seventeenth and eighteenth centuries in the wake of the wars of religion. It divides the social universe into the realm of "civil officers and magistrates" (D&C 134:3) on the one hand, who are to protect "the free exercise of conscience, the right and control of property, and the protection of life" (D&C 134:2), and religion on the other hand, where "men are amenable to [God], and to him only, for the exercise of [conscience], unless their religious opinions prompt them to infringe upon the rights and liberties of others" (D&C 134:4). Cowdery's presentation of matters is all very clean and neat and Lockean.[35] The Laws of the Church of Christ, however,

---

35. Or nearly so. While verse 5 in the current version offers an account of political legitimacy and the right of revolution that might have been cribbed from *The Second Treatise on Government*, verse 1 does make the un-Lockean claim that "governments were instituted by God" (and therefore apparently not by social contract). For an illuminating exchange on section 134, compare Frederick Mark Gedicks, "The 'Embarrassing' Section 134," *Brigham Young University Law Review* 2003/3 (2003): 959; with Rodney K.

resolutely refuses to take the easy way out offered by this settlement. Instead the Lord speaks on February 9 as though the whole medieval and early modern confrontation between divine and secular conceptions of law had never happened.

The second thing worth noting is that accommodation to the competing claims of secular sovereignty, presented in the last part of what is now section 42, is itself presented as a revealed law. For Christian and Jewish thinkers, the accommodation of divine law to the new realities of an ascendant secular law required a massive effort of exegesis and reinterpretation. It is a project with which Islamic jurists continue to grapple. This effort occurs in the commentary that surrounds the sacred text. In contrast, in section 42 the solution of retreat and compromise by divine law in the face of secular reality is not left to theologizing that takes place off the scriptural page. Rather, the accommodation and ambivalence is written directly into the divine law itself, as a revealed word. In other words, while it is tempting to read the uncompromising revelation of February 9 as the real or authentic law and the February 23 text as a retreat, it must be recognized that the February 23 text is presented as a revelation speaking in the first-person voice of God. When the deconstructed revelation that emerges from the textual history is reconstructed into the canonized text of section 42, we are left with a double-minded, almost agonistic text. Again, the history from late antiquity to the nineteenth century and from February 9 to February 23 is united in a single authoritative revelation. Both the initial indifference to competing sovereignties *and* the retreat in the face of the demands of secular jurisdictions are presented as part of one and the same divine law.

This same paradoxical approach to divine law was manifest again— and most dramatically—in the struggle over polygamy. In addition to whatever else it was, the passage of Mormonism from monogamy to polygamy and back to monogamy was a legal event.[36] While the exact

---

Smith, "James Madison, John Witherspoon, and Oliver Cowdery: The First Amendment and the 134th Section of the Doctrine and Covenants," *Brigham Young University Law Review* 2003/3 (2003): 891.

36. The best legal history of the antipolygamy battles is Sarah Barringer Gordon, *The Mormon Question: Polygamy and Constitutional Conflict in Nineteenth-Century America* (Chapel Hill: University of North Carolina Press, 2002).

origins of plural marriage within Mormonism are controversial, as a textual and scriptural matter it makes its appearance in what has become section 132 of the Doctrine and Covenants, a revelation first recorded on July 12, 1843. There the command to take plural wives is presented as a revealed "law ... instituted from before the foundation of the world" (D&C 132:5). Here again we see divine law in its most uncompromising and cosmic sense. But this law instituted before the foundation of the world soon found itself in conflict with the laws of the United States. In 1862, Congress passed the Morrill Anti-Bigamy Act, and after the Supreme Court blessed its constitutionality in 1879, the federal government loosed a hail of prosecutions and increasingly punitive legislation against the Latter-day Saints. Over the course of the 1880s, hundreds of Latter-day Saints were incarcerated, Mormon polygamists and all Mormon women were formally disenfranchised (in Idaho Territory all Mormons were deprived of the vote), and the United States began proceedings to confiscate Mormon temples and other church property.

Faced with institutional annihilation for the church and the permanent political subjugation of all Latter-day Saints, Wilford Woodruff recorded in his diary on September 25, 1890:

> I have arrived at the point in the History of my life as the President of the Church of Jesus Christ of Latter Day Saints whare I am under the necessity of acting for the Temporal Salvation of the Church. The United State[s] Government has taken a Stand & passed Laws to destroy the Latter day Saints upon the Subjet of poligamy or Patriarchal order of Marriage. After Praying to the Lord & feeling inspired by his spirit I have issued the [Manifesto announcing the end of plural marriages] which is sustained by My Councillors and the 12 Apostles.[37]

He was later to defend his actions in a sermon delivered in Logan, Utah, where he insisted, "I should have let all the temples go out of our

---

37. Susan Staker, ed., *Waiting for World's End: The Diaries of Wilford Woodruff* (Salt Lake City: Signature Books, 1993), 386–87.

hands; I should have gone to prison myself, and let every other man go there, had not the God of heaven commanded me to do what I did do."[38] Here what might appear to be a gesture of accommodation or retreat is again presented as direct revelation. Whatever the complexities of post-Manifesto polygamy, in the end plural marriage's demise in Mormon practice resulted from a claim to revelation rather than exegesis. The divine law both demanded its practice *and* suspended it.

Section 42 does not offer an entirely satisfying vision of divine law. The persistence of Mormon fundamentalism attests to the unwillingness of many to accept a divine law that claims both ultimate legitimacy and God's sanction for retreat in the face of secular opposition. The paradox lies in the fact that both the divine law instituted before the foundations of the world and the pragmatic accommodation to the "powers that be" claim divinity. The self-immolation of martyrdom in loyalty to an original revelation seems more authentic than a revealed law that in the end is willing to retreat—hence the persistence of polygamy in remote corners of the Intermountain West. The paradoxical vision of divine law presented in section 42 and dramatically enacted in the rise and fall of Mormon polygamy, however, has two major virtues. The first is the simple integrity of survival.[39] Collective martyrdom is ultimately an act of disloyalty to the community, to its continued life and existence. Section 42 provides a vision of divine law that need not end every conflict with secular authority in religious war and—given the overwhelming coercive capacity of the secular state—in defeat for the believers. The second virtue of section 42 is the unwillingness of divine law to protect itself by simply underwriting the legitimacy of secular power. By writing retreat into the fabric of divine law itself, section 42 leaves perpetually open the possibility of conflict and critique. Thus the sanctification of survival need not necessarily imply the sanctification of quietism.

---

38. "Excerpts from Three Addresses by President Wilford Woodruff Regarding the Manifesto," included in current editions of the Doctrine and Covenants alongside Official Declaration 1.

39. I borrow this phrase from a perceptive essay by Frederick Gedicks. See Gedicks, "The Integrity of Survival: A Mormon Response to Stanley Hauerwas," *DePaul Law Review* 42 (1993): 167.

Seeing section 42 as a legal text allows us to do two things. First, it gives us a model for understanding its layered textual history. Seeing scripture as law rather than the record of a sacred, revelatory event offers a reconciliation of the text's claim to authority and the way in which the authoritative text has manifestly been altered over the course of its life. Second, and more important, it provides us with a way of thinking about divine law within Mormonism. Section 42 does not present the theocratic ethic posited by some Mormon historians. Any claim to absolute ecclesiastical sovereignty is negated by the negotiation with secular law revealed in the history of the text and the shift between the February 9 portion of the text and the February 23 portion of the text, as well as the 1835 alterations to the law of consecration in order to take into account secular, legal developments. At the same time, section 42 is structured so as to challenge and reject the neat dichotomies between church and state, secular and sacred, public and private that run through modern political thought, and, one might add, the far more conventional section 134. What we are left with is a divine law that both makes claims to sovereignty and sacralizes the compromise of those claims in the face of modern legal realities. The paradox of such a divine law is precisely what allows it to both survive and claim authority for Latter-day Saints in a modern world dominated by a secular law with overwhelming coercive force.[40]

40. I would like to thank James Faulconer, Russell Arben Fox, Benjamin Huff, and Taylor Petrey for their comments and criticisms on an earlier draft of this essay. All errors, of course, remain mine.

"That My Covenant People May Be Gathered in One": The Law of Section 42 of the Doctrine and Covenants

Jeremiah John

> This is my commandment, That ye love one another, as I have loved you. Greater love hath no man than this, that a man lay down his life for his friends. Ye are my friends, if ye do whatsoever I command you. Henceforth I call you not servants; for the servant knoweth not what his lord doeth: but I have called you friends; for all things that I have heard of my Father I have made known unto you. Ye have not chosen me, but I have chosen you, and ordained you, that ye should go and bring forth fruit, and that your fruit should remain: that whatsoever ye shall ask of the Father in my name, he may give it you. These things I command you, that ye love one another. (John 15:12–17)

THE FORTHCOMING REVELATION OF THE FORTY-SECOND SECTION of the Doctrine and Covenants was announced on January 2, 1831, in Fayette, New York, about a month before it was actually received in Kirtland,

Ohio (on February 9 and 23). In D&C 38:32, the Lord declares, "Where-fore, for this cause I gave unto you the commandment that ye should go to the Ohio; and there I will give unto you my law; and there you shall be endowed with power from on high." But what is this law? Is it some new law previously unknown to the members of the church, who already had the Bible and Book of Mormon, in addition to the earlier revelations of the Prophet Joseph Smith? Is it an old law, brought to our remembrance by fresh revelation? Is it perhaps something in between, a message that weaves together ancient scripture with new promises and commandments? Of course, today members have section 42 and can read its contents and take note of its themes: the second table of the Decalogue; the consecration of goods for the poor and for the building up of the church; commandments enjoining simple dress, cleanliness, and industry; the blessings that lay in store for the faithful; and the way in which the church should deal with transgressors. But how should the form of these contents be characterized? In what sense do they constitute "The Laws of the Church of Christ"?

This paper is concerned with the meaning of *law* in section 42. My most important claim is that the Law of Doctrine and Covenants 42 is the same as the "law of Christ" referred to in Galatians 6:2 and in 3 Nephi, a law that contrasts with dominant presentations of law—as the herald of "sin and death"—in the New Testament and the Book of Mormon. In section 42, the Law consists not only of commandments, rules, and principles that govern human action, but also refers more broadly to the order of God's providential plan, including the gathering and saving work of Christ through the church. The Church of Jesus Christ of Latter-day Saints is established by revelation and by "power" sent from "on high" (D&C 38:32), as much as by the obedience and par-ticipation of those who become members. It is for this reason that the giving of the Law is closely associated with the fulfilling of prophecy (D&C 42:39), with "a great work" that the Lord has "laid up in store" (D&C 38:33), and with "mysteries of the kingdom" that are not given to the world to know (D&C 42:65). Law contains not only new com-mandments and old commandments brought to our remembrance, but also the knowledge of God's plan and his dealings with his people in the past, present, and future. This knowledge is not something added to the law but is an essential element of it, because it is only though this knowledge of God's plan that obedience to commandments gains its proper significance. By contrast, the Epistles of Paul and the Book of Mormon generally present law (specifically of the law of Moses) as a divisive, separating force that removes people from God's presence through sin and as an incomplete, disciplining set of rules that points toward Christ but cannot save without the atonement.

In the New Testament and the Book of Mormon, the law (again, specifically the law of Moses) is presented as an order that separates people from the presence of God. The law was given as a blessing, but through disobedience it became a curse. Only through Christ—not through the "works of the law"—are we justified and saved (Galatians 2:16). This theme, recurring in the Epistles of Paul, dominates the first ten chapters of Romans, where Paul teaches that "the law worketh wrath: for where no law is, there is no transgression" (Romans 4:15), and that "I was alive without the law once: but when the commandment came, sin revived, and I died" (Romans 7:9). Although the law is not wrong, it "kills" all of humanity, who will inevitably sin. The remedy for this separation, or spiritual death, is not more law or better law, but grace, obtained not through certain performances and omissions but through faith in Christ. In this way, "sin shall not have dominion over you: for ye are not under the law, but under grace" (Romans 6:14). The Book of Mormon echoes this Pauline account of law. Lehi tells his sons that there must be an opposition in all things—between happiness and misery, between good and bad (2 Nephi 2:11). But this opposition is in part created by the law and by the disobedience of human beings, who are cut off from the presence of God through the justice of the law. In his words to his son Jacob, Lehi teaches that "by the law no flesh is justified; or, by the law men are cut off," while "redemption cometh in and through the Holy Messiah" (2 Nephi 2:5–6). The law brings about punishment and misery, and only Christ can bring people to happiness—"salvation is free" (2 Nephi 2:4). In a similar vein, Alma teaches his son Corianton that salvation comes through the atonement of Christ but also that the law brings about punishment and guilt and makes possible that repentance without which mercy and grace can have no power. For Alma, the law simultaneously separates us from

God's presence and makes it possible for us to repent and receive forgiveness through Christ.

To be sure, the Book of Mormon does not contain the strong versions of the dualism between grace and law that appear in some passages in Romans and elsewhere in Paul's Epistles. In the teaching of Abinadi and Amulek, law is a necessary part of the plan of salvation, a type that points toward the sacrifice of Christ (see Mosiah 13:27–30; Alma 34:13–14). Just as Paul writes that the law was a "schoolmaster to bring us unto Christ" (Galatians 3:21–25), Abinadi teaches that it was a "very strict law" for "a stiffnecked people," designed to keep them in remembrance of their God and to serve as "types of things to come," pointing toward the sacrifice of Christ (Mosiah 13:29–31). But law in the Book of Mormon nevertheless remains connected with death, guilt, and opposition. For instance, Lehi teaches that "by the spiritual law [men and women] perish from that which is good, and become miserable forever" (2 Nephi 2:5), while Alma explains that the law brings fear of punishment and remorse (Alma 42:16–20).

All these teachings give no indication that the law is itself defective. Even Paul—who dramatically declares the blamelessness of the law to be nothing more than dung (Philippians 3:5–9)—can plainly say that the law itself is "holy, and just, and good" (Romans 7:12). Consequently, humankind is to blame, not the law, for the fact that the law kills and condemns. The relevant point here, however, is that law points entirely beyond itself. The opposition created by law looks forward to a future reunion that law itself cannot bring about. A relationship with God cannot, it appears, be a law-governed relationship. Or to put it another way, one must move beyond a law-governed relationship. The law is the good word of God, but it is also the sign of the condemnation and power that effects our separation from God. It is a rule that divides us from safety, like the flaming sword prevents Adam and Eve from partaking of the fruit of the tree of life. Law can only be overcome by what is not law.

The Doctrine and Covenants rarely refers to law in this way. To be sure, section 20, given in April 1830, recounts that God gave to human beings "commandments that they should love and serve him" but that "by the transgression of these holy laws man became sensual and devilish, and became fallen man" (vv. 19–20). To be saved, people must "repent and believe on the name of Jesus Christ" in order to receive "justification" and "sanctification," which come through "the grace of our Lord and Savior Jesus Christ" (vv. 29–31). The law is holy, but it is only mentioned in connection with the fall, while salvation in Christ is associated with faith, repentance, grace, and loving and serving God (vv. 29–31). Moreover, D&C 22, which addresses the issue of the rebaptism of converts, declares that "you cannot enter in at the strait gate by the law of Moses, neither by your dead works" (v. 2). For this reason the Lord has established the church, which is not connected to some other new law but rather with "a new and an everlasting covenant," the "last covenant" (D&C 22:1, 3). But in a revelation given in January 1831, the Lord speaks of law in a different way. He declares that his people are to be a law-governed people, that "ye shall have no laws but my laws when I come, for I am your lawgiver" (D&C 38:22). Church members are to be a "free people" with "no king nor ruler," for the Lord will be "[their] king and watch over [them]" (vv. 22, 21). The church had already been legally incorporated (according to the laws of New York) in the previous year, but here the Lord speaks further of "establishing," "gathering," and "blessing" the church by giving it law. The Lord commands: "Wherefore, for this cause I gave unto you the commandment that ye should go to the Ohio; and there I will give unto you my law" (D&C 38:32). There, endowed with power from on high (vv. 32, 38), more leaders for the church will be called (v. 34), and the people of God "shall have the riches of eternity" (v. 39). Clearly the law is no longer associated with the broken commandment by which people are condemned and separated from the presence of God. Rather, it is associated with the full establishment of the church and the gathering and redemption of Israel.

Following the pattern of section 38, later in the Doctrine and Covenants the law is used repeatedly to refer to organizing the church, gathering Israel, and bringing human beings before the Lord as "a righteous people, without spot and blameless" (cf. D&C 38:31). Section 43 speaks of the Saints receiving the law and instructing one another in it, declaring that in this way the Saints "will be sanctified by that which [they] have received" (v. 9). Section 88 even speaks of the "law of a celestial kingdom" and explains that whoever is "governed by *law* is also preserved by *law* and perfected and sanctified by the same" (vv. 25, 34). The term *law* also appears in section 88 and throughout the Doctrine and Covenants as a more general order in reference to the "law of God" (as well as to the "laws of the land" and the "laws of man") and to the laws of the various kingdoms of heaven—celestial, terrestrial, and telestial. In fact, every kingdom and all things have been given a law, for there is "no space in the which there is no kingdom" (v. 37). According to law, all things "move in their times and their seasons" (v. 42), and with every law there are "certain bounds also and conditions" (v. 38). Here the law is the government of all creation, in which human beings participate in an automatic, natural way but also through the atonement of Christ and through their voluntary faithfulness to covenants and commandments.

Of course, the Bible itself gives a few indications of this broader sense of law—not only as a set of divine commands but as the order of God's kingdom and the plan of salvation. Romans 3 sounds the more dominant perspective on law, teaching that "by the deeds of the law there shall no flesh be justified.... But now the righteousness of God without the law is manifested" (v. 20, 21). However, in Romans 8 Paul speaks of the "law of the Spirit of life in Christ Jesus [which] hath made me free from the law of sin and death" (v. 2). Similarly, in Galatians Paul explains that "no man is justified by the law in the sight of God" and that "Christ hath redeemed us from the curse of the law" (3:11, 13), yet later he is able to teach the Saints to "bear one another's burdens, and so fulfill the law of Christ" (6:2) because "all the law is fulfilled in one word, even this; Thou shalt love thy neighbour as thyself" (5:14). But what is this Pauline conception of the law of Christ (this "law of the Spirit of life in Christ Jesus"), and how is it different from the law of "sin and death"? I see two ways to draw a distinction between the two laws. First, in a narrow sense the law of Christ is the "spirit of the law," or the inward love of neighbor toward which the many outward rules of the law are directed. This law is distinct from the law of sin and death because the law of Christ focuses on inward commitment and devotion rather than on outward, potentially hypocritical performance. In this way of fulfilling the law, Paul would echo Jesus's claim in the Sermon on the Mount that the command to seek purity of heart and inward righteousness would fulfill rather than destroy the law. Second, in another sense the law of Christ could refer to the paradoxical command to love, which can only be truly fulfilled by receiving the spiritual gift of charity. The law of sin and death is the divine standard against which human beings, left to themselves, are measured and always found wanting. But the law of Christ is the divine gift of love given through the power of the Holy Spirit, a grace that gives inspiration to loving human relationships. It is in this sense that we might understand Christ's equivocation in 3 Nephi, where he teaches both that the law is fulfilled (it "hath an end") and that he himself is "the law, and the light" (3 Nephi 15:4–9).

The latter interpretation is similar to Thomas Aquinas's description of the "New Law" in the *Summa Theologica*. There Thomas argues that the New Law—the law first given in the New Testament—is chiefly "the grace of the Holy Ghost," which comes to those who believe in Christ.[1] It is this grace that fills believers with love and justifies them. The other part of the New Law, of secondary importance, is that which "dispose[s] us to receive" the grace of the Holy Ghost. This part commands not only the performance of some actions and omission of others, but also instructs believers to acquire the virtues. The New Law is the command to develop an inward orientation toward righteousness (as Christ teaches, for example, in the Sermon on the Mount), but more importantly it is the grace of God which justifies and fills with love those who believe in Christ.

This account of the New Law makes some sense of what Paul is calling the "law of the Spirit of life in Christ Jesus" in Romans 8:2. But what could it mean, generally speaking, that grace is a part of law? Grace is not a command at all, or even a rule in the usual sense, but rather a "help" or a "gift"[2] through which God prepares and directs

---

1. Thomas Aquinas, *Summa Theologica*, II-I Q. 106, A.1. There are, of course, numerous editions and translations of the *Summa*. Rather than cite a specific edition, I here use the standard notation used across all editions and translations. For a good edition, however, consult the five-volume *Summa Theologica of St. Thomas Aquinas*, trans. various (New York: Benziger Brothers, 1948).

2. II-I Q. 110, A.1.

the soul to righteousness, justifying the soul of the ungodly.[3] But grace is also, in line with Thomas's general definition of law, a "rule of reason" directed toward the common good, made by one who has care for the whole. Here a "rule of reason" does not refer only to something that directs rational beings through their deliberation and choice, but also to what governs irrational animals and even inanimate things, things that are "inclined to something by reason of some law."[4] Indeed the whole "community of the universe," not merely the human part, is governed by divine providence or "eternal law" in the sense that this community is ordered and moved according to God's rules or ordinances. The whole work of God, which directs creation to what is good, is governed by law, whether through the knowledge of rational creatures or by some "inward motive principle" that orients and moves them without their deliberate participation.[5]

If we accept that the law of Christ, the law of the celestial kingdom, and the Law of the Church referred to in Doctrine and Covenants (some of these also in parts of the New Testament) include not only commandments but the gifts of the Spirit, the saving power of the atonement, and God's preparations and help for bringing people to salvation, what does it mean that in section 42 the Lord is "giving" the law to the church? What does it mean that church members are "receiving" the law?

One thing I can say is that much of what is being given and received is not really new, at least in content. True, there are some specific instructions concerning the translation of the Bible, the procedures for dealing with unrepentant church members, the gathering of the church in the West, and most notably the practice of consecration. However, the law addressed to the church begins with a partial reminder of the Ten Commandments, specifically the commandments that concern relationships between people. Verses 18–27 of section 42 prohibit killing, lying, stealing, and adultery. The command to honor father and mother is absent, and a command to "love thy wife with all

---

3. II-I Q. 113.

4. II-I Q. 90 A.1, rep. obj. 1.

5. II-I Q. 93 A.4, 5, 6.

thy heart, and ... cleave unto her" is added, as is a general command not to "speak evil of thy neighbor, nor do him any harm." In verse 28, the Lord actually acknowledges that these are reminders, because "thou knowest my laws concerning these things are in my scriptures." But to this is added, "he that sinneth and repenteth not shall be cast out" and that "if thou lovest me thou shalt serve me and keep all my commandments" (vv. 28, 29).

This last statement is remarkable in that it is one of several equivocal (or ambiguous) "thou shalt" statements throughout section 42 that carry a connotation of promise—and therefore of grace—as well as of command. The Lord commands, "thou shalt not commit adultery" (v. 24) and "thou shalt not be idle" (v. 42), but he also declares, more prophetically, "thou shalt live together in love" (v. 45) and even "he who hath faith to see shall see" (v. 49). Indeed, many of these *thou shalt* statements emphasize the future tense with "it shall come to pass," as in the statements that "it shall come to pass, that ... every man shall be made ... a steward over his own property" (v. 32), that "it shall come to pass, that he that sinneth and repenteth not shall be cast out" (v. 37), and that "it shall come to pass, that which I spake by the mouths of my prophets shall be fulfilled" (v. 39). In these and other passages in section 42, it is not entirely clear whether the imperative or the future tense—or both—is intended, whether the emphasis lies on grace or on law. For example: "If thou lovest me thou *shalt* [*should or will?*] serve me and keep all my commandments" (v. 29); "thou *shalt* [*should or will?*] live together in love" (v. 45); and "the lame who hath faith to leap *shalt* [*should or will?*] leap" (v. 51).

This ambiguity is not just rooted in a word. I think it reflects a feature of law-governed social life itself. The law specifies what people should do. Yet wherever a law exists, people typically obey it. Is the law, then, only a regulative ideal—something people use to regulate their actions or to give them reasons to act a certain way? Or is it rather a sort of description of how they actually behave, for reasons that existed before this most recent proclamation of the law—or perhaps how they will act in the future, for reasons not wholly provided by the law itself? There is an essential relationship, I think, between these two senses of law. In any particular case, individuals may disobey the law, so it is not right to say that what is done and what is commanded are identical. Nevertheless, the Lord is not merely commanding members of the church not to harm or deceive one another. He is also promising that they (speaking of the church collectively) will live in relationships of love (v. 45), die without tasting death (v. 46), weep for those who die (v. 45), and be healed through the blessing of faith (v. 48). The Lord is also describing the relationships and practices that will exist in the church and the blessings he will bestow upon it, as he is commanding the members to participate in these practices and seek these blessings. *Receiving* the law means in this sense that the members of the church are learning to hope for and anticipate the best gifts—and indeed actually receive them.

Perhaps the most striking reference to prophecy in section 42 is in verse 39, where the Lord says that "it shall come to pass, that which I spake by the mouths of my prophets shall be fulfilled; for I will consecrate of the riches of those who embrace my gospel among the gentiles unto the poor of my people who are of the house of Israel." *But what prophecy or prophecies is this verse referring to?*[6] The clearest statement that I can find appears in Isaiah 49:22–23, a passage quoted twice in the Book of Mormon.[7]

> Thus saith the Lord God: Behold, I will lift up mine hand
> to the Gentiles, and set up my standard to the people; and
> they shall bring thy sons in their arms, and thy daughters

---

6. The February 1831 text is less clear about what exactly it is in section 42 that fulfills the prophecy but more clear about what prophecy the Lord has in mind: "[The Lord] will consecrate the riches of the Gentiles unto [his] people which are of the House of Israel." Grant Underwood, "'The Laws of the Church of Christ' (D&C 42): A Textual and Historical Analysis," in *The Doctrine and Covenants: Revelations in Context*, ed. Andrew H. Hedges, J. Spencer Fluhman, and Alonzo L. Gaskill (Provo, UT: BYU Religious Studies Center and Deseret Book, 2008), 121–22. The current text, however (while making it a bit harder to see what prophecy is referred to), makes it clear that the *fulfillment* of the prophecy is the system of consecration set up in the immediately preceding verses, specifically the consecration of the property of the rich for the maintenance of the poor.

7. Nephi quotes these verses as a part of the full text of Isaiah 49 (in 1 Nephi 21), and Jacob quotes only these verses in 2 Nephi 6:6–7.

shall be carried upon their shoulders. And kings shall be thy nursing fathers, and their queens thy nursing mothers; they shall bow down to thee with their face towards the earth, and lick up the dust of thy feet; and thou shalt know that I am the Lord; for they shall not be ashamed that wait for me. (1 Nephi 21:22–23)

Other possible antecedents include Isaiah 60:3–5, 10–12, and 14–16, which speak of Israel receiving the forces and the milk of the gentiles and predicts that the gentiles will "come to thy light" and "nurse" Israel's "daughters." Isaiah 61:5–6 speaks of strangers feeding the flocks of Israel and serving as its "plowmen and vinedressers," and the passage says that they shall "eat the riches of the Gentiles, and in their glory shall [they] boast." Isaiah 66:10–12 says that the Lord will "extend peace to [Israel] like a river, and the glory of the Gentiles like a flowing stream." The larger context of all these passages is the theme of reversal, going from weakness and obscurity to strength and glory. In this specific instance of the theme, Israel has suffered for its sins, having been punished by God through the gentiles, but in the last days the people of God will be redeemed and blessed, again by means of the gentiles. Thus, those who oppressed and hated them will admire, help, and serve them.[8]

---

8. Grant Underwood interprets Doctrine and Covenants 42:39 as a straightforward reference to Isaiah 61:6, which promises that Israel would "eat the riches of the Gentiles, and in their glory shall ye boast yourselves." But his reasons for focusing exclusively on this verse seem to be because he concentrates on an early—and as he admits, erroneous—interpretation of verse 39. The original text of D&C 42:39 did not specify that the gentiles whose riches would be consecrated would be those who "embrace [the] Gospel" and that those riches would be consecrated to "the poor of [God's] people." Because of this vagueness, some church members failed to see the connection between this prophecy and consecration, and concluded that these riches would be spoils from the wicked and the enemies of the church who would be destroyed by the wrath of God. Because of this misunderstanding, the Prophet added the clarifying words to verse 39 to specify that this fulfillment of prophecy had to do with consecration within the church, not the destruction of the wicked. See Underwood, "'Laws of the Church of Christ,'" 121–22.

By drawing a link between modern-day consecration and these ancient prophecies, readers are able to unlock new implications that are not apparent in the Isaiah verses by themselves. Section 42 enriches our understanding of the claims made by Isaiah (as well as by Nephi and Jacob) through the following teachings.

1. The gentiles spoken of in Isaiah include those who are *converted to the gospel,* who are baptized as members of the church, and who consecrate their property for the support of the poor.
2. The humbling of the gentiles and the consecration of their riches to the people of Israel do not (or do not *only*) entail a kind of tribute paid by a now-weak people to a now-strong people like spoils taken from a defeated enemy, but are rather a willing consecration of the wealth of the rich who are entering the kingdom of God.
3. The exaltation of the poor (in this context at least) occurs through their membership in the kingdom of God—indeed through their fellowship with the rich whose wealth is being consecrated to the kingdom. Thus the poor are nourished and supported as much by "Jerusalem" (or the New Jerusalem, Zion) as they are by the consecrated wealth of the rich former gentiles; the poor are blessed by the Lord, by means of the gentiles, and by means of the church and the temporal kingdom of God.

The commandments on consecration, then, appear to provide the clearest way of seeing what the Lord means when he refers to section 42 as the Laws of the Church of Christ. To receive the law is to receive the gospel, in the sense of believing the gospel and obeying the commandments and ordinances contained in it. However, it also means hearing and welcoming the good news of the work of God. The Law of the Church is the good news about gathering—it is the command to gather and prepare, but it is also the promise that the Lord himself will join his people together in love and prepare them to meet him at the temple. According to John 15, the members of the church are no longer servants who follow the commandments blindly because of fear. They are friends who rejoice in the law because they understand what God is doing (vv. 12–17). Thus the Law in Doctrine and Covenants 42 is the affirmation and explanation of the central Christian truth that the Savior is drawing all people to himself through the power of his atonement, and of the Latter-day Saint hope that the church is being led toward a common life that the Lord calls Zion.

Lon Fuller, in *The Morality of Law*, argues that the very concept of law entails an "internal morality," or a set of social and political conditions without which law cannot be called law in the true sense. Law entails a number of expectations, regularities, and coherences that make a body of rules truly law. Law that is unintelligible, in constant flux, or bears no resemblance to its application cannot be called law—not because it fails to meet a moral standard which comes from outside of law, but because it does not adhere to the everyday meaning of law and the normal way law operates in societies. Whereas John Austin argues that the presence of commands backed by threats is sufficient to constitute law, Fuller points out that commands that cannot coherently be applied to human action can hardly qualify as law, even if they provide certain perverse reasons for action. If rules contradict each other, if they are subject to constant change, if they are not publicized, or if the rules that are applied are not the same as those publicized, then they cannot constitute real law. Another way to describe this perversity is that in criminal or nonlegal regimes, the order of society bears little resemblance to the model of behavior presented by the written legal code.[9] There may be predictable ways of doing things in such a state, but they are the result of ordinary people's adjustments to the arbitrariness of the state rather than their obedience to the laws. Indeed, in such

---

9. Hegel draws a parallel between scientific and juridical law, characterizing both as a "stable image" of a phenomenon that is full of change and variation. The administration of justice is the positive, intelligible image of the human dignity of each person, which is not immediately apparent in the instrumental exchanges of these rights-bearing persons in economic life. It is through law that the true significance of associational life appears to us. See G. W. F. Hegel, *Elements of the Philosophy of Right*, ed. Allen W. Wood, trans. H. B. Nisbet (New York: Cambridge University Press 1998), sections 209–29.

societies the purpose of the action of the state is, as Fuller puts it, not "giving the citizen rules to shape his conduct, but to frighten him into impotence."[10]

Following this insight, I further conclude that while a command can fail to be law because of defective form or application, it may also fail to constitute law for reasons that have nothing to do with the lawgiver at all. The law can fail because of pervasive misunderstanding or general apostasy. A lawless society, or one where the meaning of the law is generally misunderstood, would fail to achieve the kind of reciprocity between government and subjects that Fuller claims is necessary for a kind of rule to count as law. In human history is it hard to think of an actual example of an appallingly criminal society that was governed by an upright, decent ruler and a coherent, moderate legal code. Yet this practically describes God's people throughout most of human history. In Abinadi's sermon to the priests of Noah in the book of Mosiah, misunderstanding the law and rampant disobedience are a central theme. The Jews, Abinadi explains, did not all understand the law, because of the hardness of their hearts, even though they were given a law of performances and ordinances, intended to "keep them in remembrance of their God and their duty towards him" (Mosiah 13:30). The law itself pointed toward Christ, but as Jacob had taught, they were blind to this truth because of "looking beyond the mark" (Jacob 4:14). Likewise the priests of Noah did not understand the law and the "spirit of prophesying" because they had not "applied [their] hearts to understanding" (Mosiah 12:25, 27). The people were ignorant of the law and of its true purpose because the priests had neglected to teach them.

---

10. Lon Fuller, *The Morality of Law*, rev. ed. (New Haven: Yale University Press, 1969), 40. Some social scientists have argued that corruption may actually reduce crime, since people are more afraid of crossing arbitrary officials than predictable, fair ones. The truth seems to be the opposite, however. Levels of respect for legal norms among ordinary people tend to track the levels of respect for law among bureaucrats, law enforcement officers, and judges. See Tom Tyler, *Why People Obey the Law* (Princeton, NJ: Princeton University Press, 2006); and Tom Vanderbilt, *Traffic: Why We Drive the Way We Do* (New York: Alfred A. Knopf, 2008), 235–43. In the famous story of Cesare Borgia in Machiavelli's *Prince*, Borgia appointed "the cruel and ready" Remiro D'Orco to reduce the "insolent" people of Romanga to terrified submission. But later he had to get rid of D'Orco and appoint judges in order to establish "good government."

What is the upshot of invoking Fuller's insight (and similar insights) that a ruler can fail to create law if the law is generally disobeyed or is misunderstood? It is to help readers make sense of the contrast between the Pauline and Book of Mormon presentations of law as a divisive, deadly power and the presentation of law in section 42 as a gathering and saving revelation. Paul's powerful message throughout the Epistles is that the "righteousness of the law" cannot save. The emphasis of the Book of Mormon presentation, however, is slightly different. The perverse consequences of the law come not from the limits of law itself but from failing to understand the purpose and significance of the law. Israelites "looked beyond the mark" and failed to follow the law with a hope in Christ and with the knowledge that the commandments of the law were only a part of the merciful, providential plan of God through which the people of God would be gathered together and saved through faith and repentance. The subtlety of the Book of Mormon teaching about the law of Moses (especially in Abinadi's sermon) is that "the teaching" does not drive us away from law and toward grace. Rather, it asserts that the inadequacy of the law is the failure of human beings to understand and live it properly and to see its fulfillment in Christ. In fact the message of the Book of Mormon, and even more so of the Doctrine of Covenants, is the *redemption of law* from misunderstanding and hardness of heart.

The revelation known as the Laws of the Church of Christ remedies this defect, not by presenting a new set of commands but by revealing the commandments in the context of the plan of salvation and the promises that God makes to the church. It is for this reason, I think, that the Lord speaks of receiving the law in connection with receiving "revelation upon revelation, knowledge upon knowledge" with knowing the "mysteries and peaceable things" (D&C 42:61), including "mysteries of the kingdom" (v. 65), which are not given to the world. These are the secrets of the law—truths, privately and publicly revealed, known by instruction and by lived practice, about what God has done for the people of Israel, what he is doing now for them, and what he will do in the future.

Teaching in Zion

Karen E. Spencer

DOCTRINE AND COVENANTS SECTION 42 is most known today for its discussion of the law of consecration. Early Latter-day Saints made a similar association and knew it as "The Laws of the Church of Christ." The revelation that became this section came as faithful and eager Saints had questions about their life as members of the growing church.[1] The first of their questions was simply *where* to live: "Shall the Church come together into one place or remain as they are in Separate bodies?" The answer, in verses 1–10, was to build up the church in every region for the time being. The second question was *how* to live, or, what would be the laws for the church. Above verse 11 in manuscript copies are the words "the Law regulating the Church in her present situation till the time of her gathering" or simply "the Law."[2] Verses 11–69 became the accepted set of regulations that were to govern their existence as the Lord's Saints. These verses contain the instructions that today are most readily associated with the law of consecration: they instruct Saints on how to live communally, share their excess with the poor, and begin to build a New Jerusalem to prepare for the second coming of the Savior.

---

1. See Grant Underwood, "'The Laws of the Church of Christ' (D&C 42): A Textual and Historical Analysis," in *The Doctrine and Covenants: Revelations in Context*, ed. Andrew H. Hedges, J. Spencer Fluhman, and Alonzo L. Gaskill (Provo, UT: BYU Religious Studies Center and Deseret Book, 2008), 110–14.
2. See again Underwood, "'Laws of the Church of Christ.'"

Today's Latter-day Saints sometimes feel that the section applies only loosely to them in the current church since they do not live in communal cities. For whatever reason, it seems easy to forget that Doctrine and Covenants 42 addresses more than properties and storehouses; it also discusses clothing, beauty, mourning, teaching, love, forgiveness, faith, and more. Section 42 includes all these things as important elements of a Zion community. Or put another way, understanding how to dedicate all of life to God, even clothing or mourning, prepares Latter-day Church members to become a Zion people.

This paper will focus specifically on just one of these elements: teaching. Part of my reason is that Doctrine and Covenants 42 itself gives it priority placement within the Law. Remember that the words *the law* appear just after verse 10 in many manuscripts; the first topic discussed afterwards is teaching. After a quick note in verse 11, which establishes that those preaching afar should have clear authority to do so, verses 12–14 lay out the directions concerning teaching for the Saints. These verses discuss what, how, and when (even when not) to teach. Each of these three verses is in conversation with other scriptures that help expand and explain their meaning more deeply. I will bring out those connections below. My primary aim is to show that teaching is not merely the task of relaying information in better and more effective ways. It is a profound responsibility of stewardship similar to other acts of consecration discussed throughout the Doctrine and Covenants. In this way, teaching can be an essential part of building Zion.

What to teach

> Verse 12: And again, the elders, priests and teachers of this church shall teach the principles of my gospel, which are in the Bible and the Book of Mormon, in the which is the fulness of the gospel.

The first point section 42 makes about teaching is *what* to teach. Doctrine and Covenants 42 commands that three things be considered: (1) the principles of the gospel, (2) the Bible and the Book of Mormon, and (3) the fulness of the gospel. The text also acknowledges a certain relationship between these three things: the principles of the gospel are specifically *in* the Bible and the Book of Mormon, as is the fulness of the gospel also *in* the Bible and the Book of Mormon. These two books together are a pivot point, with the principles on one hand and the fulness of the gospel on the other. The scriptures are an anchor on which teaching relies.

The scriptures themselves often model their own usability. Many places in scripture quote or allude to past scripture. Fortunately, or perhaps strategically, the very verse following verse 12 contains an allusion to a previous, significant passage; in this case, it points to an entire section of the Doctrine and Covenants. Verse 13 begins, "And they shall observe the covenants and church articles to do them." The "covenants and church articles" was, at the time, a common way to refer to what is now known as Doctrine and Covenants section 20. And in fact this section itself models teaching through the scriptures. There are references to and direct quotations from the Book of Mormon throughout this section.

The first part of section 20 contains a short history of the "rise of the church," which includes the translation of the Book of Mormon. Following this brief history is a list of doctrines confirmed by the events of the rise of the church, such as God created the earth and humans in his likeness; God gave humans commandments; transgressing these laws caused the fall; God gave his Only Begotten Son; and salvation comes to those who believe, are baptized, and endure in faith to the end. These gospel principles are all found in the Book of Mormon.[3] Here the language of section 20 does not always quote the Book of Mormon directly, but it is clearly allowing the Book of Mormon language to influence it. For example, verses 26–27 allude to several Book of Mormon passages with this same theme: "Not only those who believed after he came in the meridian of time, in the flesh, but all those from the

---

3. This was also pointed out by Ezra Taft Benson in "A New Witness for Christ," delivered at the October 1984 general conference. See Ezra Taft Benson, *A Witness and a Warning: A Modern-day Prophet Testifies of the Book of Mormon* (Salt Lake City: Deseret Book, 1988), 9–13.

beginning, even as many as were before he came, who believed in the words of the holy prophets . . . as well as those who should come after."[4]

Allusions to the Book of Mormon only become stronger as the section continues. The next part of Doctrine and Covenants 20 lays out some specifics of the new church's organization, especially the responsibilities of priesthood leaders. At least nine times phrases and words from the Book of Mormon are used, including the very language of priesthood ordinances. The most well-known and most closely quoted of these are the sacrament prayers for the bread and the water, drawn from Moroni 4:1–3 and 5:1–2 respectively. Borrowings from the Book of Mormon also include D&C 20:37 (from Moroni 6:2–3), D&C 20:45 (from Moroni 6:9), D&C 20:60 (from Moroni 3:4), D&C 20:71 (from Moroni 8:10), D&C 20:73 (from 3 Nephi 11:23–25), D&C 20:75 (from Moroni 6:6), and D&C 20:83 (from Moroni 6:7). D&C 20 is clearly intent on using the scriptures as an anchor of the new church.

One of the connections just mentioned will be particularly important later in this paper, so I will highlight it in table 1.

Table 1. Comparison of D&C 20:45 and Moroni 6:9

D&C 20:45	Moroni 6:9
The elders are to **conduct the meetings** as they are **led** by the **Holy Ghost**, according to the commandments and revelations of God.	And their **meetings were conducted** by the church after the manner of the workings of the Spirit, and by the power of the **Holy Ghost**; for as the power of the Holy Ghost **led** them whether to preach, or to exhort, or to pray, or to supplicate, or to sing, even so it was done.

Once the similarities of these verses are noted, it seems likely that D&C 20:45 is using the language of Moroni 6:9 purposefully. The main difference between the two verses is that Moroni gives more details about what the meeting might include.

---

4. See, for two examples, 1 Nephi 10:19 ("as well in these times as in times of old, and as well in times of old as in times to come; wherefore, the course of the Lord is one eternal round") and Alma 39:17 ("Behold, you marvel why these things should be known so long beforehand. Behold, I say unto you, is not a soul at this time as precious unto God as a soul will be at the time of his coming?").

Notably, not too long before Joseph Smith received Doctrine and Covenants 20, Oliver Cowdery produced a document titled the "Articles of the Church of Christ." In addition to the similarity in the names, the content of this document is so like section 20 that many scholars feel this document provided a model for D&C 20.[5] What I find most significant is that they both use a similar *method*: Oliver also used *scripture* to teach doctrines and ordinances of the restored gospel. Oliver's reasons for doing so came by revelation, but a revelation that came long before D&C 42. In 1829, the Lord said to Oliver, "Behold, I give unto you a commandment, that you rely upon the things which are written; For in them are all things written concerning the foundation of my church, my gospel, and my rock" (D&C 18:3–4). God was beginning to teach there the same principle that D&C 42:12 teaches: the scriptures are reliable and useful resources for building up the latter-day church.

We have seen so far that the first thing mentioned in the Law is teaching. We have also seen that the first thing it says about teaching is that it should focus on the principles of the gospel, as found in the Bible and the Book of Mormon. Nestled in the following verse is a reference to section 20, a section that demonstrates the potential of using the Book of Mormon when teaching about gospel principles or the foundation of the church. Verse 12 also asserts that not only the principles but even the fulness of the gospel are found there. Like D&C 18:3–4, D&C 42:12 loudly proclaims that the scriptures are comprehensive enough to rely on as we build up and teach in Zion.

---

5. Oliver's document can be reviewed in Michael Hubbard MacKay, Gerrit J. Dirkmaat, Grant Underwood, Robert J. Woodford, and William G. Hartley, eds., *Documents, Volume 1: July 1828–June 1831*, vol. 1 of the Documents series of *The Joseph Smith Papers*, edited by Dean C. Jessee, Ronald K. Esplin, Richard Lyman Bushman, and Matthew J. Grow (Salt Lake City: Church Historian's Press, 2013), 368–77. There have been several studies on the relationship between Oliver's document and section 20. I would recommend Scott H. Faulring, "An Examination of the 1829 'Articles of the Church of Christ' in Relation to Section 20 of the Doctrine and Covenants," *BYU Studies* 43/4 (2004): 57–91; and Robert J. Woodford, "The Articles and Covenants of the Church of Christ and the Book of Mormon," in *Sperry Symposium Classics: The Doctrine and Covenants*, ed. Craig K. Manscill (Provo, UT: BYU Religious Studies Center and Deseret Book, 2004), 103–16.

How to teach

> Verse 13: And they shall observe the covenants and church articles to do them, and these shall be their teachings, as they shall be directed by the Spirit.

The second point Doctrine and Covenants 42 makes about teaching is *how* it ought to be done. First, verse 13 tells Saints to "observe the covenants and church articles" (found in D&C 20), and second, to teach "as they shall be directed by the Spirit." That is, those teaching should teach according to previous commandments and according to the Spirit. Verse 12 taught that the scriptures were strong enough to rely on, but using the scriptures to teach in Zion requires a little more training. Once again, exploring the reference to D&C 20 will expand our understanding and provide some clarification.

Remember that section 20 discusses several offices of the priesthood and what duties are assigned to each office. Here in table 2 each office specifically mentioned—elder, priest, and teacher—is assigned the duty of *teaching*.

Table 2. Duties of elders, priests, and teachers

D&C 20:42 elders	**teach**, expound, exhort, baptize, and watch over the church
D&C 20:46 priests	preach, **teach**, expound, exhort, and baptize, and administer the sacrament
D&C 20:59 teachers	warn, expound, exhort, and **teach**, and invite all to come unto Christ

Thus one way of "observing" the covenants and church articles was to remember that it was a priesthood duty to teach. Failing to teach, as also failing to do any of their other duties, would mean the members of the priesthood were slackening in their efforts to build Zion.

Beyond that, however, I think there is more to be learned from the covenants and church articles about how to teach. The reference to the Spirit in D&C 42:13 may in fact refer to D&C 20:45 (see table 3). While many places in scripture exhort Saints to listen to the Spirit, the fact that D&C 42:13 refers directly to the covenants and church articles makes this allusion seem particularly likely.

Table 3. Comparison of D&C 42:13 and 20:45

D&C 42:13	D&C 20:45
And they shall observe the covenants and church articles to do them, and these shall be their **teachings, as they shall be directed by the Spirit.**	The elders are to **conduct the meetings as they are led by the Holy Ghost,** according to the commandments and revelations of God.

The language of D&C 42:13 might be a stern reminder that as elders, priests, and teachers are observing their roles, they must never forget that all this is under the direction of the Spirit. The same sentiment was also expressed in D&C 20:45, only reversed: as the elders conduct meetings by the Holy Ghost, they should remember that they are doing this according to the commandments and revelations of God.

As already noted above, Doctrine and Covenants 20:45 quotes from Moroni 6:9 (see table 1). The main difference between these two verses is that Moroni 6:9 provides greater detail than D&C 20:45. Apparently, D&C 20:45 simply abridged Moroni 6:9 for convenience, and now D&C 42:13 is paraphrasing D&C 20:45 for convenience again. However, I think a little more is going on. For instance, it turns out that most of the details Moroni included in his writings (that were dropped in D&C 20:45), actually appear in *nearby* verses in D&C 20 (see table 4).

Table 4. Comparison of Moroni 6:9 and D&C 20:42, 46, 59

Moroni 6:9	D&C 20:42, 46, 59
for as the power of the Holy Ghost led them whether to **preach,** or to **exhort**, or to pray, or to supplicate, or to sing, even so it was done	teach, expound, **exhort**, baptize, and watch over the church
	preach, teach, expound, **exhort**, and baptize, and administer the sacrament
	warn, expound, **exhort**, and teach, and invite all to come unto Christ

The details Moroni gives are specific examples of what the Holy Ghost might direct them to do (preaching, exhorting, praying, supplicating, and singing), and as just noted, these or similar words are found throughout the descriptions of the duties of the elders, priests, teachers, and deacons.

Coming full circle, Moroni 6:9 helps us see that when D&C 42:13 reminds elders, priests, and teachers that they should "observe" the covenants and church articles, they are being reminded of two things at the same time: they are being reminded of their responsibility to teach and also of their responsibility to conduct the *entire meeting* by the Spirit. That is, they should keep in mind that teaching might or might not be what the Holy Ghost is leading them to do. This responsibility means that they will at times be directed to teach and at other times to exhort, sing, and so on. Therefore, read in this light, the word *as* in the phrase "as they are directed by the Spirit" means "if" they are directed to teach, or "inasmuch as" they are directed to teach.

To review, verse 12 opened this passage by directing that what should be taught are the principles of the gospel, with an eye to the Bible and the Book of Mormon. Verse 13 followed this up by using Doctrine and Covenants 20 to explain how teaching is related both to the priesthood and to other things that happen when the Saints gather together. Most importantly, verse 13 emphasizes that in all these commandments, the leader is the Spirit.

When to teach

> Verse 14: And the Spirit shall be given unto you by the prayer of faith; and if ye receive not the Spirit ye shall not teach.

The last point Doctrine and Covenants 42 makes about teaching is *when* to teach. There are three important details here. The first is that the Spirit comes *when* you ask for it "by the prayer of faith." The second detail is only implied but is a bit surprising: even if you ask, the Spirit might not come. And the third detail can certainly be rather uncomfortable: if it does not come, "ye shall not teach."

Both in the early days of the Latter-day Saint Church as well as today, this verse is one of the most commonly quoted verses in talks and books about teaching.[6] Hundreds of LDS talks use this verse to

---

6. There are several dozen references to this verse in Brigham Young University's online scripture index, an index that tracks references to scriptures in public discourses

encourage teachers to pray for the Spirit so that their teaching might be as effective as possible. There are often discussions as well on how ineffective it is to teach without the Spirit. In fact it is used so often that Elder Dallin H. Oaks said that the words of this verse, along with D&C 50:13–14 and 21–22, are "so familiar they are almost slogans." He went on to warn: "We are in danger of using them without understanding them."[7]

I think what might be missing in Latter-day Saint discussions of this verse is some explanation of the last, uncomfortable detail: without the Spirit "ye shall not teach." The image of a teacher abandoning the lesson and sitting in silence is so awkward that discussions usually simply do not address this part of the verse at all. (One exception is the interpretation that a teacher without the spirit is talking but not really *teaching* anything.) Certainly the most *important* detail is clear in these talks: the Spirit is crucial to teaching. And understandably, that has been, and will continue to be, the focus of talks meant to inspire teachers. For the purposes of this paper, however, I would like to expand on the question of how this last detail might be interpreted in a way that is productive to teachers.

Verse 14, like verse 13, is concerned with when the Spirit will or will not lead one to teach, but verse 14 uses slightly different language: that of "receiving" the Spirit. At the time section 42 was given, there was a question among religious Americans about what it meant to "receive" spirits in general. And as Mark Staker has made clear, Kirtland was not immune from these questions.[8] Converts, neighbors, and visitors brought to Kirtland ideas from various traditions. Among these traditions was a group called the "Shouting Methodists," who, like others, took spiritual manifestations as a central aspect of worship. The name they gave to their experiences with the Holy Ghost was getting "the power." Staker explains, "Shouting Methodists and other

of the LDS Church from the time of Joseph Smith up through the present. Only a few early references, found in the *Journal of Discourses*, take the idea seriously that there might be a time to not teach. The index can be accessed at http://scriptures.byu.edu/.

7. Dallin H. Oaks, "Teaching and Learning by the Spirit," *Ensign*, March 1997, 7.

8. See Mark Lyman Staker, *Hearken, O Ye People: The Historical Setting for Joseph Smith's Ohio Revelations* (Salt Lake City: Greg Kofford Books, 2009).

religious enthusiasts expected that 'the power,' meaning the power of God or the Holy Spirit, would come as they prayed, causing them to fall to the ground, binding their tongues, making it impossible to speak, and sometimes accompanying these manifestations with jerks and trembling."[9]

It is worth pointing out here how closely this resembles Joseph Smith's story about his own religious experiences. Joseph says in his history that he grew up in a time of "great excitement" where ministers were "getting up and promoting this extraordinary scene of religious feeling, in order to have everybody converted, as they were pleased to call it" (JS—H 1:8, 6). Staker brilliantly compares what happened to Joseph Smith just before the first vision with what others were calling "the power": "No sooner did he kneel and begin to offer up the desires of his heart to God, than he was 'seized upon by some power.' It was 'the power of some actual being from the unseen world who had such a marvelous power as I had never before felt.' His consistent description of the force as a 'power' used a word and described effects familiar to Shouting Methodists since it 'entirely overcame' him in such a way that it could 'bind' his tongue."[10]

Many in Kirtland were seeking after this very experience during the time when Doctrine and Covenants 42 was received. There were also many in Kirtland who were uneasy about this sort of religious expression. Several of the elders asked Joseph Smith to inquire of God what was right and wrong. One might expect that Joseph would not have needed to ask God, since he had gained wisdom from his own experiences. However, when the elders asked him to give inspired clarification, he decided to again "ask of God" (JS—H 1:13) and received, as part of this clarification, what is now sections 46 and 50. Each of these sections deals with receiving the Spirit and the danger of receiving what *seems* to be divine manifestations but what is actually the work of false spirits. These sections served to greatly clarify the Saints' understanding and will assist us in comprehending D&C 42:14.

9. Staker, *Hearken, O Ye People*, 135.
10. Staker, *Hearken, O Ye People*, 135–36.

Doctrine and Covenants 46 repeats a commandment from section 20: "The elders ... [shall] conduct all meetings as they are directed and guided by the Holy Spirit" (v. 2). (It's almost as if it is set out to prove that this is a continuation of the trajectory running through Moroni 6, D&C 20, and D&C 42.) Verse 7 repeats this idea, but pushes beyond to the question at hand: "That which the Spirit testifies unto you even so I would that ye should do in all holiness of heart, walking uprightly before me, considering the end of your salvation, doing all things with prayer and thanksgiving, that ye may not be seduced by evil spirits, or doctrines of devils, or the commandments of men; for some are of men, and others of devils."

This verse acknowledges the possibility that some in Kirtland have been, or could be, confused about their spiritual experiences. In order to avoid this confusion, Doctrine and Covenants 46:7 exhorts members to do "all things with prayer" and to do this in "holiness of heart." The following verses add to this, suggesting that another way to avoid confusion is to remember that spiritual gifts are not a mark of superior spirituality. For example, while the elders have the assignment to conduct meetings by the Spirit, the members are also commanded to seek the Spirit (v. 7) and also to "seek ... earnestly the best gifts" (v. 8). In addition, both leaders and general members should not seek for "a sign that [individuals] may consume it upon their lusts," but rather for spiritual gifts from which "all may be benefited" and "all may be profited" (vv. 9, 12). These verses confirm the liberality of the Spirit's gifts, given to "every man," but they also warn that these gifts are not given for selfish purposes. Perhaps one of the major misunderstandings in Kirtland was that Saints were seeking spiritual manifestations such as "the power" to show off their superior spirituality.

In addition, Doctrine and Covenants 46 emphasizes that these gifts are "given unto the church" (v. 10). That is, these gifts are given to individual members of the church, so that other members of the church may be blessed. This is akin to the way Paul talks about spiritual gifts in 1 Corinthians: "Forasmuch as ye are zealous of spiritual gifts, seek that ye may excel to the edifying of the church" (1 Corinthians 14:12). Not only are these gifts not meant to be proof of spiritual uniqueness or superiority, they also are not meant to be used just for the individual.

In fact, many of these gifts are only able to be used if they are received when other people are present. For example, "To some it is given by the Holy Ghost to know that Jesus Christ is the Son of God, . . . [and] to others it is given to believe on their words" (D&C 46:13–14). Another example: "To another is given the word of knowledge, that all may be taught to be wise and to have knowledge" (v. 18). Note that even the gifts of healing and being healed (verses 19 and 20) require at least two people: one who needs to be healed, and one who can do the healing.[11] This is also like Paul's direction to not speak in tongues unless another is able and *present* to interpret (1 Corinthians 14:27–28).

We have seen three points about gifts so far in Doctrine and Covenants 46: they can be sought by all members, they should not be used for prideful reasons, and they are often received in a group setting. Reading section 46 this way, one could see this discussion of spiritual gifts as similar to the discussion about conducting meetings in Moroni 6:9 or D&C 20. Just as the Spirit guides the person conducting a meeting, the Spirit also oversees the distribution of spiritual gifts. And these two things come together, since the members in a meeting of a congregation and the member conducting that meeting are all being guided by the same Spirit. Remembering that all are potential participants and all are to be benefited helps members avoid pride and therefore avoid seduction by evil spirits.

All of this is helpful, but it does not quite address the original question: how can the Saints tell if a spiritual gift they are receiving is from God? Or, further, what if there are those "among you professing and yet be not of God" (D&C 46:27)? The response in section 46 is that a "head" is required to oversee spiritual manifestations, language again similar to that of Paul.[12] Even though the previous verses just

---

11. The command to gather first before revelation comes is present elsewhere in scripture. For example, see Doctrine and Covenants 6:32 and Matthew 18:20, which state that "where two or three are gathered together in my name, there am I in the midst of them."

12. The word *head* may be building again on Paul's teachings. After a list of spiritual gifts in 1 Corinthians 12, Paul says, "But all these worketh that one and the selfsame Spirit, dividing to every man severally as he will. For as the body is one, and hath many members, and all the members of that one body, being many, are one body: so also is

suggested an equality about spiritual gifts (they are given to every man, severally) Doctrine and Covenants 46:27–29 explains that "the bishop of the church, and ... elders unto the church, are to have it given unto them to discern all those gifts ... [and] unto some it may be given to have all those gifts, that there may be a head." Once it is understood that all can receive spiritual gifts, we return to the idea that someone is at the head to "conduct" those gifts and see where the Spirit is leading them as a group. At this point, the section folds back on itself to the words in verse 2 that "it always has been given to the elders of my church ... to conduct all meetings as they are directed and guided by the Holy Spirit."

However, those assigned to leadership positions in Kirtland were apparently still left confused about just how to perform this responsibility. Doctrine and Covenants 46 did not condemn any specific spiritual manifestation, something that would have made it easier for leaders to identify those who were "not of God." As Staker explains, since the revelation left decisions up to the membership, most Saints simply continued on as they had before.[13] Only when further clarification came, in what is now D&C 50, did their understanding begin to change.[14]

Among other things, section 50 confirms that some of the Saints in Kirtland were receiving evil spirits. Verses 13–15 and 17–18 include this stern rebuke:

Christ" (vv. 11–12). A head is the part of the body that conducts the others. It sees what the other parts are doing and decides what should be done with them. To emphasize the connection between *head* in verse 29 and Paul's image of the *body of Christ*, the first time that D&C 46 actually uses the word *member*—which Paul uses throughout his discussion—is in verse 29. It says, "That unto some it may be given to have all those gifts, that there may be a head, in order that every member may be profited thereby."

13. See Staker, *Hearken, O Ye People*, 137.

14. It is worth mentioning that although things *began* to change with section 50, it was really the June Conference—held just a month later—that ended the debate on spiritual gifts. At this conference, there were those who received "the power," and Joseph or others cast the devil out of those persons. It became clear, over and over again, which manifestations were of the Spirit and which were not. For the purposes of this paper, however, I limit my focus to the instruction in section 50 on how to discern spirits and how it compares to D&C 42:12–14.

> Wherefore, I the Lord ask you this question—unto what were ye ordained? To preach my gospel by the Spirit, even the Comforter which was sent forth to teach the truth. And then received ye spirits which ye could not understand, and received them to be of God; and in this are ye justified? ... Verily I say unto you, he that is ordained of me and sent forth to preach the word of truth by the Comforter, in the Spirit of truth, doth he preach it by the Spirit of truth or some other way? And if it be by some other way it is not of God. (D&C 50:13–18)

The problem in Kirtland was that the elders *thought* they were teaching and conducting with the Spirit, but had instead mistaken other spirits for the Holy Spirit. Section 50 warns that "there are many spirits which are false spirits, which have gone forth in the earth" (v. 2). Even though they were teaching "the word of truth" (perhaps even following D&C 42:12 by teaching the principles of the gospel from the scriptures), they were receiving and teaching by spirits that they "could not understand" and that were "not of God" (see also D&C 46:27). And as in D&C 46, section 50 also gives all members the responsibility to distinguish spirits: "And again, he that receiveth the word of truth, doth he receive it by the Spirit of truth ... ? If it be some other way it is not of God" (D&C 50:19–20). Section 50 broadens this responsibility to all members, teachers and hearers alike.

However, after this equal responsibility is affirmed, D&C 50 returns to the idea that someone needs to be at the "head." This time the person is given the authority not only to discern spirits but to command them:

> But know this, it shall be given you what you shall ask; and as ye are appointed to the head, the spirits shall be subject unto you. Wherefore, it shall come to pass, that if you behold a spirit manifested that you cannot understand, and you receive not that spirit, ye shall ask of the Father in the name of Jesus; and if he give not unto you that spirit, then you may know that it is not of God. (D&C 50:30–31)

And now, finally, we come back to the language of Doctrine and Covenants 42:14. To help illuminate the connection with these passages, see table 5.

Table 5. Comparison of D&C 50:31 and 42:14

D&C 50:31	D&C 42:14
Wherefore, it shall come to pass, that if you behold a spirit manifested that you cannot understand, and you receive not that spirit, ye shall **ask of the Father in the name of Jesus**; and **if he give not unto you that spirit,** then you may know that it is not of God.	And the Spirit shall be given unto you by the **prayer** of faith; and if ye **receive not the Spirit** ye shall not teach.

While not identical in nature, the principle in both seems the same. In both cases, the person (the head of a congregation or classroom) is instructed to proceed according to the Spirit. In both cases, if there seems to be a spirit present, then the person should pray for the Spirit, by the prayer of faith. If the spirit (or Spirit) is withheld, then the person can know that that feeling or spirit was not of God.

If this is a fair interpretation, then it would seem that a person who is called upon or who desires to teach should seek out the Spirit by the "prayer of faith." If the Spirit comes, then the person can proceed to teach. If it does not come, then the teacher is directed "not [to] teach" because it is not what God wants in that instance. Teaching at that moment would be without the aid of the Spirit and therefore by "some other way." Not only would that be "less effective," as is commonly identified, it would also be "not of God." The strictness of the command that "ye shall not teach" may imply that some teachers will be tempted to continue to teach without the Spirit and claim that their words are God's words.[15]

This may still seem a bit abstract or, at worse, to leave teachers terrified of teaching when they should not feel that trepidation. (I can see why most talks do not address this verse directly.) However, when Doctrine

---

15. I realize this language sounds harsh, and I admit that I do not always know when I myself am listening to the Spirit. I take comfort in D&C 50:16: "Behold ye shall answer this question yourselves; nevertheless, I will be merciful unto you; he that is weak among you hereafter shall be made strong."

and Covenants 42:12–14 are taken as a whole, the instruction is actually much more robust. Remember that the above discussion of verse 13 showed that the Spirit may push toward exhortation, supplication, singing, teaching, and so forth. A person authorized as a teacher for a given classroom may feel guided to do any of these things, as before mentioned. Verse 14 comes at this same principle from a different angle. A teacher who studied the scriptures and came prepared to teach may, in the moment of teaching, feel the Spirit leave or lessen. In that moment, as the Spirit withdraws a pace, the teacher has the choice of *not teaching* according to the plan. The opportunity is then opened for the teacher to listen for where the Spirit is directing and go that way instead. A teacher who has been praying for the Spirit in faith, and who has been authorized to be at the head of a classroom, has the right and responsibility to pay attention to when the Spirit is there and when it withdraws. By this care, a teacher can fulfill her or his role outlined in D&C 42:12–14.

Stewardship

The Doctrine and Covenants envisions church members as stewards over their properties. That is, they are not in actuality the owners of their belongings but those that oversee and take care of them. God is the owner of the earth, and the Saints are his servants. D&C 42:32 says, "Every man shall be made accountable unto me, a steward over his own property, or that which he has received by consecration." In a parallel way, the Doctrine and Covenants asks members to receive other aspects of their lives by consecration: their clothing, their relationships with friends and family, their food, their health habits, and more. Essentially, everything, even the air we breathe, is God's and given to human beings to use.[16]

Teaching is, in a sense, also an opportunity to receive a stewardship by consecration. God gives teachers scriptures that are full of God's words as well as wisdom he gave to the prophets. God also provides a gathering place where members associate with one another. And those associations are organized by the relationships of teachers and students,

---

16. See King Benjamin's discourse in Mosiah chapters 2–4.

or leaders and members, given through callings. A person who is called to be a teacher is called as a steward over a certain space and time, with the assignment of teaching the principles of the gospel, according to the directions of the Spirit. Teachers offer up their might, mind, and strength, and, like other consecrated offerings, they do it unto God.

In order to illustrate this further, bear with me as I write more casually as if I were training a newly called leader in a ward Young Women program.

> Joseph Smith revealed to early Latter-day Saints a law in Doctrine and Covenants 42 about how to live together as Saints. A lot of it deals with the law of consecration and property, but it also talks about consecrating other things, like teaching. So today I want to share with you what I see D&C 42:12–14 tells us about teaching gospel principles.
>
> Verse 12 says to teach the principles of the gospel that are in the Bible and the Book of Mormon. It also says that these scriptures have the fulness of the gospel. I love the idea that they have both the fulness and the principles, both the deeper and more complex things as well as the simple basics. The instructions in our teaching materials say to use the outlines or manuals as *suggested* guides or resources to help us teach, but they also say that the primary foundation for all that we are teaching is the scriptures themselves.
>
> Talks by apostles and general leaders can be great examples of how to do this. These women and men have searched the scriptures diligently and know how to teach the gospel from them. In addition, using their talks in class can help the young women see how to read and understand scriptures better. These leaders have also allowed themselves to be changed by scripture, so you can often see the principles of the gospel coming through their life stories.
>
> As your young women have questions, don't feel like you need to know all the answers. Remind them that they can find answers in the scriptures and through the Holy Ghost. That is kind of a leap of faith, for them and for us, but I encourage you to trust that they can find answers this way.

Verse 13 reminds us that we should be "directed by the Spirit" when we lead and teach. I encourage you to have faith that God really can send the Holy Ghost to guide you. Sometimes you'll feel the Spirit when you are thinking about the topic you're going to teach, or you'll have ideas of how to present something. Also, sometimes you'll feel guided by the Spirit in the classroom to do something you hadn't planned on. In the Book of Mormon, Moroni talks about how they handled their church meetings. He says when elders conducted by the Spirit, sometimes they were led to preach, exhort, pray, supplicate, or sing. When you're teaching, try to be open to the Spirit pushing you to do something you hadn't planned on. You might feel impressed to *exhort* the young women to keep a commandment just discussed in the scriptures. You might feel impressed to allow for some silent time to *pray* or ponder. You might ask them to think of the words to a song or even ask the class to *sing*. So even though we say it's lesson time, really any of these things can be part of teaching a lesson. It's up to you to listen to the Spirit and respond to his direction.

Also, watch for how the Spirit might be prompting the young women during your lesson. I've watched some lessons where a girl's answer was overlooked because it didn't match the wording of the answer in the manual. I think she was genuinely seeking to understand scripture, but she came away distrusting her ability to learn on her own and listen to the Spirit. You might not expect that to be a problem when there are not manuals, except that we might still have an idea in our heads of what the girls should say in response. But instead, it's exciting to think that the young women can teach us too. D&C 50 says the teacher and the student should be edified together when the Spirit is there. And D&C 46, which lists a lot of spiritual gifts, talks about how gifts are meant to be shared with each other.

Verse 14 in D&C 42 is a little tricky. It says that the Spirit comes by the prayer of faith, but it also says that sometimes the Spirit won't come. Apostles have pointed out that sometimes God doesn't tell us what to do because he wants us to make decisions and grow. When we pray for the Spirit and nothing seems to stop us, then I think we should feel confident in moving forward. But I've also had times where I can tell that what I'm doing or planning to do just isn't quite right.

For example, once I had prepared to teach a lesson to help my young women learn something from 2 Nephi. I had pondered the lesson, and I was excited to have a lively discussion with them. But when I got into the classroom, it seemed like the girls were quieter than usual. It was hard to get conversation going about the lesson. In that moment I said a quick prayer, and I decided to ask the girls what they were thinking about. It turned out that several of them were bothered by current world events and how they would affect them personally. We switched gears and addressed their concerns as a group. The lesson flowed, and the girls were comforted. God has promised to send us the Spirit when we teach, so feel free to pray for it before and during your lessons.

There is just one last thing I want to mention—a temptation that we can have as teachers. Don't feel that you need to teach like someone else does. Just make your calling something that you and God are doing together. You can watch or talk to other teachers to get ideas, of course, but some people are tempted to think that if someone is a good teacher then they should just imitate how they teach. But it isn't the *methods* of a teacher that make them a good teacher—it's actually the Spirit. (And remember that the Spirit doesn't always make someone cry. The gifts of the Spirit come in many different ways, like feeling enlightened, uplifted, or comforted. You may have seen a teacher once who tried to manufacture the Spirit by making their lesson overly emotional. That's a pretty dangerous and really audacious thing to try. But what's sad too is that they don't need to work on that—the Spirit will do the real work.)

In summary, trust the scriptures and pray for the Spirit. Trust that God has a work he is after, and remember also that he trusts you! He has given you a stewardship to watch over and teach young women—*his* young women. As you give your time and efforts, he will give in return all the gifts of the Spirit you need to fulfill your stewardship.

Concluding thoughts

The "Laws of the Church of Christ" were a law for creating Zion. As part of that Zion city, teaching is seen as a stewardship, just like a stewardship of land or property. Teachers labor in Zion by studying the scriptures, reading, pondering what to teach, thinking, questioning, praying for the Spirit's guidance, and loving their students. This labor yields fruits of knowledge, plans, outlines, ideas, wisdom, joy, testimony, and ability to understand the needs of students. All that the teacher has produced is brought to the moment of teaching, and in that moment the Spirit can choose to return these fruits back to the teacher to use in the lesson or to send other means, including the gifts of the Spirit. Seen from this point of view, teaching is another form of the law of consecration.

Elder Oaks has been concerned that the words "teaching by the Spirit" have become a slogan, and warns that there is a danger in using them like that. It seems to me that the greatest danger is that by using these words casually, members may miss the fact that Zion can actually be built. Some members assume that Zion is a place far away in the past or far away in the future. The Saints in 1831 were given this law not because they were in Zion already but because they were to build it.

When Nephi discusses Zion he points directly to the teachers. He mourns over teachers who "preach and set themselves up for a light unto the world, that they may get gain and praise of the world." Because these will not "labor for Zion," Zion, along with them, will "perish" (2 Nephi 26:29–31). In Zion, teaching cannot be done for praise. Nothing can be done for the praise of the world. No matter what the members of the church are consecrating, yielding to the directions of the Spirit instead of to the praise of the world is the basis of consecration.

As Brigham Young put it, "Whenever we are disposed to give ourselves perfectly to righteousness, to yield all the powers and faculties of the soul ... ; when we are swallowed up in the will of Him who has called us; when we enjoy the peace and the smiles of our Father in Heaven, the things of His Spirit, and all the blessings we are capacitated to receive and improve upon, then are we in Zion, *that is Zion*."[17]

---

17. Brigham Young, "Salvation," in *Journal of Discourses*, 1:3, emphasis in original.

"Thou Wilt Remember the Poor": Social Justice and a Radical Reading of "The Laws of the Church of Christ" (Doctrine and Covenants 42)

Russell Arben Fox

THE STRUCTURE OF MY BASIC ARGUMENT hinges upon explicating several principles that are important to the social justice teachings of the Catholic and Reformed Christian traditions. These principles include solidarity and equality, personalism and distributism, and the preferential option for the poor. It is my claim that Joseph Smith's revelation of the laws of consecration and stewardship, as first articulated through the oft-revised and rearranged text "The Laws of the Church of Christ," may be understood as providing normative support for all of these principles. In short, I believe Doctrine and Covenants 42 should be read as a social justice document, one supportive of economic approaches conducive to these aims.

It is of course rather radical, not to mention audacious, to take a text composed nearly 170 years ago by Joseph Smith (and possibly some others),[1] produced through a process that those disposed to take the Doctrines and Covenants seriously would assume to have involved some sort of revealed language or guidance from God, and subject it to a reading that wrests support from a political, economic, and religious platform about which Smith himself almost certainly knew nothing whatsoever. So be it. My aim is merely to explore a reading, not to definitively express a meaning. The practical historical record of the early Saints' various attempts to live the laws of consecration and stewardship is vital to understanding it. This means looking closely at the practices and explanations that arose in response to both the Laws of the Church of Christ (in both its 1831 original and its 1835 revised versions) in Ohio and Missouri, as well as at the sermons preached and the policies implemented by church leaders regarding the establishment of a "United Order of Enoch" in Utah during the 1870s. But this vital historical record is not, I think, the sole or deciding contribution to readers' understanding of the revelation. Some acts of hermeneutical interpretation aim to recover an objective meaning of the text; my interpretation aims to examine the language of the text under consideration so as to express and speculate about its possible applications.[2] That those possibilities are ones that I am, personally and politically, sympathetic to does not undermine the validity of my suggestions. The readers' own prejudgments are inseparably a part of what they bring to any reading, and sometimes it is those prejudices that make

---

1. As Grant Underwood observes, the phrase "as agreed upon by seven Elders," which appears in the early Ryder manuscript of the revelation linking the February 9 section of the text to the February 23 section, suggests "something more than mere ratification of what Joseph Smith received.... It is possible that the seven elders played an active role in helping the Prophet define the procedures recorded that day." Grant Underwood, "'The Laws of the Church of Christ' (D&C 42): A Textual and Historical Analysis," in *The Doctrine and Covenants: Revelations in Context*, ed. Andrew H. Hedges, J. Spencer Fluhman, and Alonzo L. Gaskill (Provo, UT: BYU Religious Studies Center and Deseret Book, 2008), 112.

2. For the philosophical ideas guiding me here, see Charles Taylor, "Language and Human Nature," in *Human Agency and Language: Philosophical Papers 1* (New York: Cambridge University Press, 1985), 215–47.

possible some speculative approach that might otherwise never have been attempted.[3]

To be fair, some have argued that, as the fundamental message of any text that has been collectively accepted as "scripture" by the membership of the church is dependent upon the guidance of "the living oracles" of the church, the only form of interpretation with any kind of legitimacy would be one that turns to the writings of the presently sustained prophets and apostles and that attempts to identify "the inchoate normative logic" of the "practices and institutions" they currently direct.[4] Doing so in connection with the laws of stewardship and consecration arguably suggests a strong denial of the appropriateness of approaching section 42 by way of a social justice reading. For example, church leaders of both the present and the recent (as opposed to nineteenth-century) past have given numerous and often vehement defenses of free market economics and condemnations of organized labor and welfare policies.[5] Moreover, some of those closer to the original reception of the Laws of the Church of Christ have emphatically denied the notion that the communitarianism suggested by the revelation was a form of "Socialism" or "French Communism."[6] It is worth noting, however, that when these early church leaders disavowed any connection between such systems and the laws in question, they were mostly referring to the anarchist and communalistic experiments in the tradition of Pierre-Joseph Proudhon, Robert Owen, and others, which were quite different from what the social justice tradition teaches. Also worth noting is that the interpretation of the early

3. For more on this argument, see Hans-Georg Gadamer, "The Problem of Historical Consciousness," in *Interpretive Social Science: A Reader*, ed. Paul Rabinow and William M. Sullivan (Berkeley: University of California Press, 1979), 148–52 and passim.

4. Nathan B. Oman, "'The Living Oracles': Legal Interpretation and Mormon Thought," *Dialogue: A Journal of Mormon Thought* 42/2 (2009): 3–6 and passim.

5. See Duane Boyce, "Do Liberal Economic Policies Approximate the Law of Consecration?" *FARMS Review* 21/1 (2009): 197–213; and Phillip J. Bryson, "In Defense of Capitalism: Church Leaders on Property, Wealth, and the Economic Order," *BYU Studies* 38/3 (1999): 89–107.

6. John Taylor, *The Government of God* (London: Latter-day Saint Book Depot, 1852), 23; and Lorenzo Snow, "United Order, Etc.," in *Journal of Discourses*, 19:349.

church's experiments with communitarian economics that focused fiercely upon distinguishing such practices from twentieth-century state socialism and communism was likely driven far more by the ideologically shaping global political realities that confronted leaders like J. Reuben Clark and Ezra Taft Benson than by a thorough knowledge of the actual history of those experiments.[7] Indeed, the argument can be made that the relative absence of social-justice-friendly prophetic readings of the laws of consecration and stewardship was more a historical accident than anything else.[8]

But even given all these caveats, I believe my argument is worth consideration. Not only am I not suggesting the recovery of an original or objective meaning of the revelation in question, but I am not even seeking to develop a reading of the text that aspires to any binding legitimacy upon the faith of members of the church. This is, first and last, an act of speculation and persuasion, nothing more. I would argue that such open-ended speculation, when confronted with as influential and as ambiguous a text as the Laws of the Church of Christ, particularly the principles of consecration and stewardship first articulated therein, is the only reasonable response. Two Latter-day Saint scholars wrote, years ago, that while gospel teachings do not "outline a theory of economic justice . . . in any operational manner," the principles contained within the revelations—principles that, among other things, "condemn the ostentatious consumption of the rich and encourage Saints to care for the poor"—make it incumbent upon members "to struggle with the dilemma of economic justice."[9] These scholars were following the argument made by church leaders from Brigham Young to Marion G. Romney, who claimed that the Lord "has not the least objection" to his children, in all times and in all places, attempting to

---

7. James W. Lucas and Warner P. Woodworth, *Working toward Zion: Principles of the United Order for the Modern World* (Salt Lake City: Aspen Books, 1996), 132–33, 140–42, and passim.

8. Ethan Yorgason, "No Grounds for Conversation: The Regional Construction of Fundamental Differences between Mormonism and Socialism," *Antipode: A Radical Journal of Geography* 34/4 (2002): 707–29.

9. James R. Kearl and Clayne Pope, "The Church in the Secular World" (lecture, Brigham Young University, Provo, UT, 1975; copy in possession of author).

construct the United Order of Enoch and that "the united order," in all its various versions and applications, is "the gospel in its perfection" and should be the goal "toward which we move."[10] Writing this essay is an act of adding my voice in support of one additional, frequently beleaguered possible route toward the achievement of that goal.

Principles of social justice

While the teachings on social and economic justice within the Catholic and Reformed Christian traditions are enormously broad and multi-faceted, such teachings can be fairly accurately summarized through the following three interlocking moral demands.[11]

1. *Solidarity and equality.* Within social justice thought, the equal dignity and respect of persons are seen as dependent upon, and a function of, tightly bound and mutually supporting communities who share two overarching aims. The first is providing for the essential needs of those who lack the civil liberties, material resources, education, health care, or opportunities for work by which dignity is made possible; and the second is maintaining the integrity and balance of the community that its members identify with, thereby enabling the degree of trust and solidarity that supporting and sacrificing on behalf of one another require.

2. *Personalism and distributism.* Any true esteem of one's fellow person is inseparable from a prior granting to him or her the ability to freely labor and develop in a mutually beneficial and personally satisfying vocation. Consequently, as important as guaranteed rights to individual persons are, an economic system that (to a degree) levels and distributes property and work opportunities through

---

10. Brigham Young, "The Order of Enoch, Etc.," in *Journal of Discourses,* 16:8; and Marion G. Romney, "Welfare Services," *Ensign,* November 1975, 124.

11. These points are adapted from documents that may be accessed from the website for the Center for Public Justice (http://www.cpjustice.org/) and the Office for Social Justice (http://www.osjspm.org/default.aspx).

stewardships, apprenticeships, and the like is also essential to the maintenance of the common good.

3. *Option (or "preference") for the poor.* This final moral demand, unlike the prior ones, does not partake of an argument about forms of social organization; hence, the demand is not as directly relevant to what may be drawn from Smith's writings and the tradition of consecration and stewardship. But that does not minimize its enormous moral importance as a declaration that—in the midst of tending to all other political, economic, and social matters of concern to individual persons and communities—the *centrality of the poor* must be constant. The poor, weak, disadvantaged, and suffering will always have a prior moral claim on the conscience of financially stable members of the church, and all decisions should be made with the standpoint of keeping in mind the needs of the powerless and weak.

The aim of the remainder of this paper will be to present my case for reading the Laws of the Church of Christ as being supportive of, or at least suggestive of, these basic principles.

Solidarity and equality

The textual linking of solidarity and equality in the revelations composed by Joseph Smith begins even before the Laws of the Church of Christ were received. On January 2, 1831, at the third conference of the church, Smith gave "a revelation to guide and instruct the church" to the members assembled together in the home of Peter Whitmer Sr. in Fayette, New York.[12] That revelation, which eventually became Doctrine and Covenants 38, set the stage for subsequent egalitarian thinking among early members by issuing at least two crucial edicts. First, the whole body of the church was to relocate to Ohio—a prospect that prompted "divisions among the congregation" and required "great

---

12. As recollected by Orson Pratt, "Union of Spirit and Sentiment, Etc.," in *Journal of Discourses*, 7:372.

sacrifices of property"[13]—where, the Lord declared, "I will give unto you my law" (D&C 38:32). Second, this relocation, and presumably the sacrifice it entailed as well as the promised law which it would result in, both depended upon and necessitated a high degree of unity among members of the church: "Let every man esteem his brother as himself.... If ye are not one ye are not mine" (vv. 25, 27). The poor members of the congregation were to be assisted in making this journey, and all members, regardless of their calling in the church, were to equally give of the "labor of [their] hands"; the result would be a prepared and covenanted community, mild and meek, separated out from the wicked, with all things gathered "unto the bosom of the church" (vv. 38–42).

A month later, Smith and others had made the move to Ohio. To whatever degree the state of a prophet's mind is important to understanding the inspired texts that such individuals create, Smith was likely influenced at this time by other events. He had his work on his "New Translation" of the Bible—which began with Genesis in the summer of 1830 and by December of that year had brought him to the story of Enoch and the city of Zion, in which all were "of one heart and one mind, and dwelt in righteousness" with "no poor among them" (Moses 7:18–19).[14] He was also aware of the "Family," a communalistic order of Christians attempting to live according to the precepts of Acts 2:44–45 (a passage that describes early Christians living in close proximity to each other and having "all things common"), centered around the farm of Isaac Morley outside Kirtland. They practiced a rough communism of all possessions, and the experiment exercised significant influence over both the members of and those sympathetic to the young LDS Church in that part of Ohio.[15] These and other matters are likely to have

---

13. John Whitmer and Newel Knight, both cited in Lyndon W. Cook, ed., *The Revelations of Joseph Smith* (Salt Lake City: Deseret Book, 1985), 56.

14. See *History of the Church*, 6:57; and Robert L. Millet, "Joseph Smith's Translation of the Bible: A Historical Overview," in *The Joseph Smith Translation: The Restoration of Plain and Precious Things*, ed. Monte S. Nyman and Robert L. Millet (Provo, UT: BYU Religious Studies Center, 1985), 27–28.

15. See Mark Lyman Staker, *Hearken, O Ye People: The Historical Setting for Joseph Smith's Ohio Revelations* (Salt Lake City: Greg Kofford Books, 2009), 37–48, 93–118, and passim.

complemented Smith's thinking as he petitioned the Lord on February 9, 1831, for direction in how to organize the faithful Latter-day Saints. In response to a question put to him regarding "the Law regulating the Church in her present situation till the time of her gathering," Smith dictated several passages dealing with the authority to teach and reiterating the biblical commandments against murder, theft, and adultery. He then gave the following:

> If thou lovest me thou shalt serve me & keep all my commandments and behold thou shalt consecrate all thy property that which thou hath unto me with a covenant & deed which cannot be broken and they shall be laid before the Bishop of my Church & two of the Elders such as he shall appoint and set apart for that purpose and it shall come to pass that the Bishop of my Church after he has received the properties of my Church that it cannot be taken from you, he shall appoint every man a steward over his own property or that which he hath received inasmuch as it shall be sufficient for himself & family and the residue shall be kept to him that hath not, that every man may receive according as he stands in need, & the residue shall be kept in my Store House to administer to the poor & needy as shall be appointed by the Elders of the Church & the Bishop & for the purpose of purchasing lands & the building up the New Jerusalem which is hereafter to be revealed that my Covenant people may be gathered in me in the day that I shall come to my Temple this do for the salvation of my people and it shall come to pass that he that sinneth and repenteth not shall be cast out and shall not receive again that which he hath consecrated unto me for it shall come to pass that which I spake by the mouth of my prophets shall be fulfilled for I will consecrate the riches of the Gentiles unto my people which are of the House of Israel and again thou shalt not be proud of heart, let all thy Garments be plain & their

> beauty the beauty of the work of thine own hands & let
> all things be done in decency before me.[16]

In this early version of the revelation, there is an awareness of the poor—"him that hath not," "the poor and needy," and so forth—that is very much in line with the statements composed by Smith earlier in New York (in what is now section 38). However, the primary focus of this passage is clearly the building up of a self-sufficient, separate, and simple devotional—or what has come to be called an "intentional"—community.[17] The goal is to create a covenant people that will be gathered to the Lord's temple and receive salvation, a people that will give all that they have to the achievement of this end and consider this giving an all-or-nothing proposition, one that is suggestive of the parable of the ten virgins. If a member disobeys the commandments or otherwise is cast out for unrighteousness, all that has been devoted to the community stays with the community, and any opportunity for the individual to benefit from or share in that which had been consecrated is lost.

The reason for this firmness was the desire to see all members of the church "on an equal economic footing, considering their respective family obligations, circumstances, needs, and 'just wants.' ... The system aimed at equality in consumption but not in the capital controlled or managed by individuals."[18] In other words, a degree of sacrifice, consecration, and redistribution was commanded of the Saints, not to achieve a perfect economic equality among them but to give them grounds for *living together as rough equals.* It was not imagined that all would produce equal amounts of goods and services nor that all would

---

16. In H. Michael Marquardt, *The Joseph Smith Revelations: Text and Commentary* (Salt Lake City: Signature Books, 1999), 108–9.

17. See Rosabeth Moss Kanter, *Commitment and Community: Communes and Utopias in Sociological Perspective* (Cambridge, MA: Harvard University Press, 1972).

18. Leonard J. Arrington, Feramorz Y. Fox, and Dean L. May, *Building the City of God: Community and Cooperation among the Mormons*, 2nd ed. (Urbana: University of Illinois Press, 1992), 16. The reference to "just wants" comes from Doctrine and Covenants 82:17, which is part of a revelation received on April 26, 1832, in Independence, Missouri.

manage their affairs in the same way. But all members of the church community would consecrate their property to the whole church, accept the rule of recognizing the proper limits of their own and their family's needs and concerns, content themselves with life within those circumscribed limits defined by the stewardship they were assigned, and donate whatever surplus came from their individual labors and genius to the whole once again. The particular focus on dignity, respect, mutual support, and coexistence is made even clearer in the specific phrasing of a call for equality among the Saints in a revelation that Smith dictated a month later. In a wide-ranging set of statements regarding the relations between the sexes and between human beings and the natural world, the word of God was that "it is not given that one man should possess that which is above another, wherefore the world lieth in sin" (D&C 49:20).

Too often, the understanding associated with the teachings of social justice, and whatever elements of leveling and redistributing it may entail, is one that turns on the impossible quest to achieve perfect equality among all members of a society. That this flawed understanding has taken root so broadly is perhaps understandable since the legacy of totalitarian governments and fanatical cults using equality as a club to oppress and destroy individual differences is so widespread. Nonetheless, the fact remains that the central concern of almost all serious efforts to construct mutually supporting communities is not, and has never been, simple, strict economic equality. This is clearly manifest in the Catechism of the Catholic Church,[19] as well as—perhaps surprisingly—in the writings of Karl Marx. For him, the central normative problem with capitalism was not the poverty or powerlessness of the

---

19. "The equality of men rests essentially on their dignity.... 'Talents' are not distributed equally. These differences belong to God's plan, who wills that each receive what he needs from others, and that those endowed with particular 'talents' share the benefits with those who need them.... Excessive economic and social disparity between individuals and peoples of the human race is a source of scandal, and militates against social justice, equity, human dignity, as well as social and international peace.... [Thus is the] principle of solidarity ... a direct demand of human and Christian brotherhood." "Equality and Differences among Men" and "Human Solidarity," *Catechism of the Catholic Church* (http://www.vatican.va/archive/catechism/p3s1c2a3.htm).

proletariat or the inequality between the classes. The central problem was alienation—a feeling of separateness from one's own work and one's own fellow man.[20] Although capitalism in its fullest modern sense was only still emerging on the American frontier in the early 1830s, I would argue that it was, in essence, this problem of alienation that Smith aimed to resolve. The community of Saints would support one another, "live together in love" (D&C 42:45), and treat others as equals and with respect (which included paying for whatever one received from another as a service or an exchange, v. 54). Thus none would have the kind of social power over another that uncircumscribed economic expansion and consumption unfortunately makes possible.[21] Instead, social power would be shared, allowing individual members of the Latter-day Saint community with their mutually determined steward-ships (the bishop to whom members' properties would be consecrated, as well as the whole body of the church) to be sources of mutual counsel and consent. The end result would be a system that granted both per-sonal dignity and an equality in "social status ... , the esteem, deference or prestige connected with one's position in the social order."[22]

In reflecting upon this principle in later years, Brigham Young knew clearly that the point was never to create an economic uniformity of property or talent among the Saints.[23] The point was to create a social equality, wherein the differences between rich and poor were mitigated and all could enjoy a degree of solidarity with one another. No prophet has stated this better than Lorenzo Snow did:

---

20. This is best detailed in Marx's essay "On the Jewish Question." In that essay, his sole reference to equality is a somewhat contemptuous one that sees the obsession with equal rights or equal treatment as incapable of appreciating the collective problem of alienation created by industrial capitalism, instead contenting itself with the goal of describing every person as "equally ... a self-sufficient monad." See Karl Marx, *Selected Writings*, ed. Lawrence H. Simon (Indianapolis: Hackett, 1994), 17.

21. This is another reference to Karl Marx, this time to the Communist Manifesto: "Capital is, therefore, not a personal, it is a social power." Marx, *Selected Writings*, 170.

22. A. Don Sorenson, "Being Equal in Earthly and Heavenly Power: The Idea of Stewardship in the United Order," *BYU Studies* 18/1 (1977): 111.

23. See Brigham Young, "The United Order, Etc.," in *Journal of Discourses*, 18:353–54.

Zion cannot be built except on the principles of union required by celestial law. It is high time for us to enter into these things. It is more pleasant and agreeable for the Latter-day Saints to enter into this work and build up Zion, than to build up ourselves and have this great competition which is destroying us. Now let things go on in our midst in our Gentile fashion, and you would see an aristocracy growing amongst us, whose language to the poor would be, "we do not require your company; we are going to have things very fine; we are quite busy now, please call some other time." You would have classes established here, some very poor and some very rich. Now, the Lord is not going to have anything of that kind. There has to be an equality; and we have to observe these principles that are designed to give every one the privilege of gathering around him the comforts and conveniences of life. The Lord, in his economy of spiritual things, has fixed that every man, according to his perseverance and faithfulness, will receive exaltation and glory in the eternal worlds–a fullness of the Priesthood, and a fullness of the glory of God. This is the economy of God's system by which men and women can be exalted spiritually. The same with regard to temporal affairs.[24]

Snow's combination of the temporal and the spiritual, the economic and the heavenly, was typical of the rhetoric of consecration and stewardship throughout the nineteenth century. In social justice terms, this rhetorical approach demonstrates the belief that earthly solidarity and equality make possible the greater extension of charity and Christian love. George Q. Cannon expressed it thus, reflecting in 1882 on the church's history of experiments with the principles of stewardship and consecration:

---

24. Snow, "United Order, Etc.," in *Journal of Discourses*, 19:349.

> Watch the effect of wealth.... Communities get wealthy
> and they begin to think about their wealth. Where their
> treasure is there is their heart also. Especially is this the
> case if they are divided into classes.... If we are nearly
> alike temporally we feel alike. In this has consisted
> much of our strength in the past. We were not divided
> into classes, with interests diverse one from another....
> The increase of wealth, therefore, and the consequent
> increase of fashions are more to be dreaded than hostile
> legislation.[25]

The emergence of classes—of the different interests that characterize
those who are greatly diverse in relative amounts of personal wealth—
is something the principles of stewardship and consecration were
designed to prevent. The strength of the church depended upon the
application of such principles.

Personalism and distributism

The traditions of the Catholic and Reformed churches by and large
dissent from both classical liberalism and orthodox Marxism in their
accounts of the individual. In contrast, these mostly continental Euro-
pean Christian traditions developed in response to the extensive and
frequently violent cultural transformations and conflicts during the
nineteenth and early twentieth centuries, a conception of the person
that posited the individual as a bearer of rights as well as being essentially connected to an organic community. The human personality, an
endlessly varying expression of God's diverse gifts to his creation, is
inseparable from the historical, natural, and economic development of
the social world wherein that personality may articulate itself. Owing
some debt to both phenomenology and existentialism, personalism is
one way of expressing the Hegelian insight into *Sittlichkeit*, the "ethical life" of organic associations that makes possible the structures of

---

25. George Q. Cannon, "Opposition to the Saints, and Its Cause," in *Journal of
Discourses*, 24:46–47.

human consciousness.[26] The Christian authors most responsible for developing the idea range from Max Scheler and Martin Buber to Jacques Maritain and Karol Wojtyla (better known as Pope John Paul II).[27] Probably the most influential personalist text, however, made no direct reference to the doctrine; rather, it was a paper encyclical that spelled out what a just personalist response to economic life ought to be: Pope Leo XIII's *Rerum Novarum*.

Often considered alongside Pius XI's *Quadragesimo Anno*, John XXIII's *Mater et Magistra*, and Paul VI's *Populorum Progressio* as one of the essential documents of Catholic social justice teaching, *Rerum Novarum* ("Of New Things") contemplated the accelerated specialization of labor and concentration of capital that had attended the Industrial Revolution, with the consequent emergence of a largely propertyless, often exploited, wage-earning class. Such an economic existence, Leo believed, would almost certainly make impossible the full and Christian development of the human personality, since it carried with it a separation from the kind of dependable foundation that an organic connection to one's work and one's place enables. Consequently, *ownership* of one's own means of economic livelihood, if possible, becomes essential. As Allan Carlson writes:

> The pope declares the first duty of the state to be the safeguarding of justly held private property. The "great labor question" facing the modern era could not be solved except by acknowledging "that private ownership must be held sacred and inviolable." Most observers see this statement as a rejection of socialism. It is surely that, but it is also much more. For *Rerum Novarum* urges that the law "should favor ownership, and its policy should be to induce as many as possible of the people to become owners.... If working people can be encouraged to look

---

26. See part 3, "Ethical Life," of G. W. F. Hegel, *Elements of the Philosophy of Right*, ed. Allen W. Wood, trans. H. B. Nisbet (New York: Cambridge University Press, 1991).

27. A good summary of this body of thought can be found in John F. Crosby, *The Selfhood of the Human Person* (Washington, DC: Catholic University of America Press, 1996).

forward to obtaining a share in the land, the consequence will be that the gulf between vast wealth and sheer poverty will be bridged over, and the respective classes will be brought nearer to one another." In short, the crafting of a society based on small property, particularly in land, becomes the Catholic solution to the modern industrial crisis.[28]

To follow this recommendation through completely, however, would require a reversal of the enormous gains in overall wealth that capitalist development—and the attendant concentrations of property and resources—had generated over the previous two centuries. Leo did not imagine such a reversal (unlike more agrarian-minded reactionaries)[29] and recognized that, where property-based solutions of deprivation and alienation were not viable, at the very least a reconsideration of the organic connection with one's community that a decent wage makes possible was in order. Carlson explains, "Arguing that 'the present age handed over the workers, each alone and defenseless, to the inhumanity of employers and the unbridled greed of competitors,' Leo rejected the wage theory of liberalism that considered wage just which resulted from a free contract between employer and worker."[30] The answer had to involve union action, pressures upon corporations and government to ensure the provision of a "family wage," and demand for the collective providing of public goods (such as public education and universal health care) that otherwise would be priced outside the reach of many family breadwinners. All these can be included under the general title "distributism."

Distributist thought has had relatively few defenders in the century and a half since *Rerum Novarum*; instead, it has been mostly

---

28. Allan C. Carlson, *Third Ways: How Bulgarian Greens, Swedish Housewives, and Beer-Swilling Englishmen Created Family-Centered Economies—and Why They Disappeared* (Wilmington: ISI Books, 2007), 7–8.

29. See, for example, Jeffrey Marlett, "Harvesting an Overlooked Freedom: The Anti-Urban Vision of American Catholic Agrarianism," *Sources of Social Reform, Part Two* (Fall 1998): 88–108.

30. Carlson, *Third Ways*, 158.

marginalized as a presumably implausible protectionist, pseudo-agrarian, or Luddite response to the wealth-creating logic of industrial and finance capitalism. The creative destruction of the material constituents of one form of life so as to make room for a better one, the mobility of the labor force, the profit motive, the constant reliance upon debt and credit, the omnipresent commercialization of ordinary needs, the two-income family, the economic pressures and rewards attending to the ideal of constant meritocratic advancement—all these have been essentially embraced in the contemporary world. The dominant alternatives to this kind of "mere capitalism" have been some form of liberal egalitarianism (which takes as settled the nature of human market transactions and seeks to mollify their consequences through individual payments and transfers of one sort or another) or some variety of state socialism (wherein the market is controlled and directed toward predetermined ends). The notion of a decentralized system of property and income redistribution, one that nonetheless takes with great seriousness the individual inputs into that which has been distributed—which is essentially what a personalist economics calls for—has few advocates. Fortunately for the purpose of this paper, many of the most outspoken are Latter-day Saints, though they did not recognize their arguments as such.

The idea of distributing the opportunity for individual ownership far and wide was central to the laws of consecration and stewardship. After some discussion with John Finch, a disciple of Robert Owen who visited Nauvoo in September 1843, Joseph Smith reiterated that the key difference between the plan outlined in the Laws of the Church of Christ and other communalistic experiments common in America at the time was that, under the United Order, "every one is a steward over his own."[31] Was this an accurate response? Perhaps it was not under the first attempts to live the laws of consecration and stewardship in 1831 and 1832, during which time property was expected to be formally deeded to the bishop, who would then work out a "stewardship agreement" with the consecrating member; this did, in fact, "limit tenure on

---

31. Scott H. Faulring, ed., *An American Prophet's Record: The Diaries and Journals of Joseph Smith* (Salt Lake City: Signature Books, 1989), 415.

property."[32] By 1833—at least partly as a result of a lawsuit brought by a member named Bates who sought to recover his consecrated properties, but perhaps also as a result of Smith's own further reflection upon the issue—the matter was clarified: Smith wrote to Edward Partridge, the man called to be bishop and thus responsible for developing stewardships, in a letter dated May 2, 1833:

> Concerning inheritances, you are bound by the law of the Lord, to give a deed, securing to him who receives inheritances, his inheritance, for an everlasting inheritance, or in other words, to be his individual property, his private stewardship, and if he is found a transgressor & should be cut off, out of the church, his inheritance is his still and he is delivered over to the buffetings of satan, till the day of redemption, But the property which he consecrated to the poor, for their benefit, & inheritance, & stewardship, he cannot obtain again by the law of the Lord.[33]

The insertion of specific language about consecrated properties being defined as for the benefit of the poor may be interpreted as a means employed by Smith and perhaps other church leaders to avoid lawsuits. As Underwood writes, "Because charitable donations were legally safeguarded in a way that communal resource sharing was not, ... wording was added to similarly clarify that the poor were the specific beneficiaries of consecrations."[34] But perhaps too much can be made of this change in wording. The real heart of the change was in emphasizing that stewardships for which church members had responsibility really *were* their own property. This made the work of determining such stewardships, and the amount of "surplus" or "residue" to be consecrated to the bishop, more complicated—that much is certain. A letter from Joseph Smith dated June 25, 1833, reflected on this: "Every man must be his own judge how much he should receive

---

32. Dean L. May, "The Economics of Zion," *Sunstone*, August 1990, 19.

33. Marquardt, *Joseph Smith Revelations*, 113; see also Lyndon W. Cook, *Joseph Smith and the Law of Consecration* (Provo, UT: Grandin Book, 1985), 20–21, 29–30.

34. Underwood, "Textual and Historical Analysis," 120.

and how much he should suffer to remain in the hands of the Bishop" (speaking here to "those who consecrate more than they need for the support of themselves and their families"). At the same time, though, for the individual member to "say how much he needs and the Bishop obliged to comply with his judgment is to throw Zion into confusion and make a slave of the Bishop." Thus was a "balance or equilibrium of power" needed—and if one could not be developed, then a higher committee of church leaders would have to get involved, and so forth.[35] Don Sorenson observes that this additional level of interaction, imposed upon the original, much more simple, direct, and absolute vision of consecration expressed in the 1831 text, need not be understood as the further bureaucratization of the program; rather, in bringing additional players and responsibilities to bear on any act involving the consecration and distribution of property, it may be understood as the sort of preparatory interactions—guided by "harmony and good will"—that make members capable of being "equal in the bonds of heavenly things.... Our schooling in equality here is preparatory for a place of equality hereafter."[36]

One point remains. Even if it is accepted that the laws of consecration and stewardship replicate the social justice principle of distributism (by providing for a system of economic stewardships that aim to give every working member a dependable economic base to contribute to the community and enjoy full personal dignity), what is the case when there is no land to distribute? Leo's original distributist vision clearly presumed some sort of minimal agrarian foundation upon which the faithful could build, and in fact this was the case for early members of the Church of Jesus Christ of Latter-day Saints. Could the LDS articulation of this principle operate in nonagrarian, more specialized contexts? John A. Widtsoe, for one, thought so. Picking up on the conflation, from 1833 and onward, of the terms *stewardship* and *inheritance*, he wrote:

---

35. Letter cited in Underwood, "Textual and Historical Analysis," 124–25.
36. Sorenson, "Being Equal in Earthly and Heavenly Power," 109–10.

> Each member would receive a sufficient portion, called an "inheritance," from the common treasury, to enable him to continue his trade, business or profession as he may desire. The farmer would receive land and implements; the tradesman, tools and materials; the merchant, the necessary capital; the professional man, instruments, books, etc. Members who work for others would receive proportionate interests in the enterprises they serve. No one would be without property—all would have an inheritance.[37]

This idea of stewardships incorporating a distribution of inheritances—which could include capital investment, educational supports, or vocational apprenticeships—is suggestive of a host of contemporary egalitarian or social democratic policies and proposals, ranging from the Perpetual Education Fund in the church today to various plans to establish a common stakeholder fund that provides members of the community with an original purchase upon the organic life of the society in which they live.[38] However one chooses to pursue the idea, it points in the direction of the social justice tradition: a response to economic alienation and deprivation that is premised on neither liberal rights nor Marxist categories, but rather on the development of the person through collective action taken to preserve the moral and educational worth of laboring on property or in a field of one's own.

The preferential option for the poor

As mentioned above, events from 1831 through 1833, in both Kirtland and Missouri, led to some rethinking of how best to express and act upon the principles that Smith originally presented as the Laws of the

---

37. John A. Widtsoe, *Joseph Smith: Seeker after Truth, Prophet of God* (Salt Lake City: Bookcraft, 1957), 193.

38. There are a great many forms that any such stakeholder proposal may take, depending first of all on if one is speaking of a large, national community or a smaller, intentional one. In either case though, Bruce Ackerman and Anne Alstott, *The Stakeholder Society* (New Haven: Yale University Press, 1999), is the place to begin exploring the idea.

Church of Christ. This rethinking and revising, which had apparently begun as early as late 1831, was mostly completed from September 1834 through September 1835, which was when the first version of the complete Doctrine and Covenants was published.[39] In that published version, the relevant portions of the revelation read as follows:

> If thou lovest me thou shalt serve me and keep all my commandments. And behold, thou wilt remember the poor, and consecrate of thy properties for their support, that which thou has to impart unto them, with a covenant and a deed which cannot be broken—and inasmuch as ye impart of your substance unto the poor, ye will do it unto me—and they shall be laid before the bishop of my church and his counselors, two of the elders, or high priests, such as he shall or has appointed and set apart for that purpose.
>
> And it shall come to pass, that after they are laid before the bishop of my church, and after that he has received these testimonies concerning the consecration of the properties of my church, that they cannot be taken from the church, agreeable to my commandments, every man shall be made accountable unto me, a steward over his own property, or that which he has received by consecration, inasmuch as is sufficient for himself and family.
>
> And again, if there shall be properties in the hands of the church, or any individuals of it, more than is necessary for their support, after this first consecration, which is a residue, to be consecrated unto the bishop, it shall be kept to administer to those who have not, from time to time, that every man who has need may be amply supplied, and receive according to his wants.
>
> Therefore, the residue shall be kept in my store house, to administer to the poor and the needy, as shall be appointed by the high council of the church, and the

---

39. Underwood, "Textual and Historical Analysis," 113.

> bishop and his council, and for the public benefit of the
> church, and building houses of worship, and building up
> of the New Jerusalem, which is hereafter to be revealed,
> that my covenant people may be gathered in one in that
> day when I shall come to my temple. And I do this for the
> salvation of my people.[40]

First and foremost, the line "remember the poor" is different in this version of the revelation. Then, following it, the purpose of consecration is changed somewhat. Now the faithful are commanded to impart some portion of their property explicitly to the support of the poor. Of course, this is folded into the general Christian understanding that acts of charity toward the poor and the needy are comparable to serving the Lord directly ("inasmuch as ye impart of your substance unto the poor, ye will do it unto me"). This folding-into continues later in the revelation, with the idea of using the residue of consecrated properties (after stewardships had been assigned to the faithful) not simply to "administer to the poor and the needy" but also "for the public benefit of the church"—a possibly innocuous addition, but one that nonetheless appears to express considerably more expansive language than the more enclosed, borderline apocalyptic tone that the revelation adopted originally. It may also be worth noting that the earliest version speaks of members of the community receiving only that which is necessary to their full participation in the work to be done ("every man may receive according as he stands in need"), while the subsequent version seems more aware of the pluralism inherent in the collective desires of the faithful, stating that every man will be "amply supplied" and will "receive according to his wants." (The language of "just wants," as contained in the 1832 revelation of Doctrine and Covenants 82, is not present in this formulation.)

There are, of course, many ways to read these changes, some of which have already been alluded to (legal challenges to the church, etc.) and others that I have avoided discussing because of my desire to focus on the ideas expressed by the Laws of the Church of Christ

---

40. Marquardt, *Joseph Smith Revelations*, 111.

rather than on accounts of their historical implementation. But I would like to concentrate, as a conclusion to this paper, on that first central change—remembering the poor—and what it has to say about the relationship between the principles of stewardship and consecration, and social justice principles generally.

Probably no other task occupied more of Smith's time during the years 1831–1833 than his New Translation of the Bible. The bulk of the work on that project was essentially finished by July of 1833, by which time Smith had read back through and had frequently elaborated at great length upon numerous scriptural stories and passages. However, what might be most relevant here was not the changes he made to the biblical text but what he got out of that rereading. As is well known, one of the most common themes found in the Bible, both the Old and New Testaments, is the care of the poor. "Remember the poor" is a direct quotation of Galatians 2:10, and the call to remember the poor, to rescue them from oppression, and to provide relief for their suffering is echoed in literally hundreds of verses throughout the Bible.[41] To think about the needs of those who go without is an arguably related but still significantly different task than thinking about the needs of the faithful who have accepted baptism and are committed (at least ideally) to the principle of consecration within a closely defined, mutually supportive community. To think about the poor as a category of persons obliges the boundaries of the relevant community to be reconsidered and broadened.

There was an another change to Smith's thinking as well. By 1833, he was speaking not just of a New Jerusalem but of "stakes" of Zion, Zion being no longer simply a promised location in Missouri but an elastic concept that would, while still centered in a specific locale, extend and include a far greater range of particular congregations than the original 1831 revelation could reasonably be read to accommodate. I would suggest that Smith's expanding vision of Zion prompted him, along with the aforementioned intense engagement with the repetitive

---

41. See Ron Sider, *Rich Christians in an Age of Hunger: Moving from Affluence to Generosity* (New York: Thomas Nelson, 2005); and S. Michael Wilcox, *What the Scriptures Teach Us about Prosperity* (Salt Lake City: Deseret Book, 2010), for just a beginning to the many expressions of this central theme throughout the scriptures.

calls to serve the poor contained throughout the Bible, to reorient the abiding goal of what became Doctrine and Covenants 42: to make it an outline of an economic order that would conscript all the faithful into a joint, charitable project, aimed at providing succor to the poor in general as well as building up the church's infrastructure. The expanded presumptions—perhaps slightly less intensely communal yet slightly more open to individual activity and variation—behind the kind of community these verses refer to hint at larger aims for consecration than purely devotional purposes.

This strikes me as a promising way to appropriate the message of the Laws of the Church of Christ for our present moment, wherein such tremendous wealth has been generated through globalized markets that average levels of income and living are raising around the globe, though that average hides an increasingly steep gap separating the wealthy and the powerful from the marginalized and suffering.[42] As a far-flung community of believers, living in the midst of diverse yet (thanks to globalization) mostly market-related economic structures and surrounded in most countries by huge divides between the rich and the poor, members of the LDS Church today have no truly likely practical options available to them in terms of socioeconomic consecration, enclosure, and community building. The era of the United Order as experimented with during the Utah period is clearly past, to say nothing of what the Saints attempted in 1831–1833. However, if members think about becoming a covenant people in terms of forming, through the stakes (including primarily fellow members, but also reaching out to all those who live within stake jurisdictions) and local associations and cooperatives that aim to build up public resources and serve the poor, they would be following the path that, upon my reading, captures the heart of what the finalized version of these verses claim the Lord wanted his people to do. This is the church as (what

---

42. See Dan Andrews and Andrew Leigh, "More Inequality, Less Social Mobility," *Applied Economics Letters* 16/15 (2009): 1489–92; Jonathan Heathcote, Fabrizio Perri, and Giovanni L. Violante, "Unequal We Stand: An Empirical Analysis of Economic Inequality in the United States, 1967–2006," *Review of Economic Dynamics* 13/1 (2010): 15–51; and John Hills, Tom Sefton, and Kitty Stewart, eds., *Towards a More Equal Society?: Poverty, Inequality and Policy since 1997* (Bristol: Policy Press, 2009).

Erik Olin Wright would call) an "interstitial institution," a nonstate agent that does not claim to act with the authority of a state nor denies the relevance of such to achieving social justice ends, but acts instead as a contributor to the state by presenting a "consciously constructed form of social organization that differs from the dominant structures of power and inequality [in capitalist society]."[43]

Of course, further revelations may, in time, change or reorient this way of thinking about community and the power of the church to become fully unified despite the immense growth and change that has been experienced since Smith's day. And moreover, such thinking obviously does not address how members ought to act as citizens in their respective polities to achieve similar ends or at least make the achievement of said ends more likely. But I am doubtful that section 42 can be taken to provide such specific socioeconomic guidance anyway. It is, after all, a document that, even as it has gone through revisions, seems overwhelmingly shaped by a political-theological position that rejects existing authority and anticipates the construction of something new in order to receive the coming of the Lord. The point of closely investigating the history and language of the revelation is, rather, to gain an anticipatory perspective on that newness—a new set of arrangements that, I would argue at least, tends toward an emphasis upon social justice. What readers do with that perspective is an entirely different question from the one that the revelation was originally presented as answering (though a worthy question all the same).

---

43. Erik Olin Wright, *Envisioning Real Utopias* (London: Verso, 2010), 324 and passim.

Consecration, Holy War, and the Poor: An Apocalyptic Approach to Doctrine and Covenants 42

Robert Couch

FOR REASONS THAT WILL BECOME CLEARER as my argument progresses, I aim here to provide an *apocalyptic* interpretation of Doctrine and Covenants 42. But what does this mean? In an article proposing a Latter-day Saint perspective of "apocalyptic theology," LDS theologian James Faulconer claims that "the Apocalypse does not so much refer to the end of the world ... as it refers to the moment when the nearness of the kingdom of God is revealed to the believer and the believer's life is oriented by that kingdom rather than by the world."[1] If this is right, and apocalyptic scriptural themes should be understood as a means of helping the reading community orient itself to God's kingdom rather than to the world, then it is obviously of utmost importance to understand what "the world" refers to. This is a central question for any interpretation of section 42, focused as it is on marking boundaries that differentiate the Zion community from the world.

What, then, is the world? One popular interpretative possibility for a modern audience is to understand the world primarily with reference

---

1. James Faulconer, "Rethinking Theology: The Shadow of the Apocalypse," in *Faith, Philosophy, Scripture* (Provo, UT: Neal A. Maxwell Institute Press, 2010), 109–36.

to secularism—the world is the secular world. Certainly, in debates between secularists and religionists there is often a lack of consensus regarding first principles. But there are reasons to be suspicious of any claim that religion has nothing to do with the secular world. Secular German philosopher Jürgen Habermas, for instance, has suggested that a human rights framework comprises a "general and rationally motivated" basis for moral principles, amenable to the "universalism of morality as natural law" adhered to by religions.[2] Religious natural law theorists, for their part, argue that the apparently religious principles from the second tablet of the Decalogue can be recognized or discovered by anyone, religious or secular, who is willing to follow the dictates of rational thought.[3] Such points of contact make it difficult to draw too sharp a distinction between religion and the so-called secular world.

Doctrine and Covenants 42, in the course of presenting divine law, focuses heavily on supposedly secular concerns—to the point that it lists second-tablet injunctions against murder, stealing, lying, and adultery, but without any mention of first-tablet commandments (those that regulate the relationship between the spiritual community and its God). The vision of the New Jerusalem presented in section 42 does not seem primarily concerned with differentiating itself from secularism, at least not from versions of secularism that are friendly to the humanistic values found on Moses's second tablet.[4]

---

2. Jürgen Habermas, "Israel and Athens, or to Whom Does Anamnestic Reason Belong? On Unity in Multicultural Diversity," in *Liberation Theologies, Postmodernity, and the Americas*, ed. David Batstone, Eduardo Mandieta, Lois Ann Lorentzen, and Dwight N. Hopkins (New York: Routledge, 1997), 251–52.

3. For a recent discussion, see William E. May, "Contemporary Perspectives on Thomistic Natural Law," in *St. Thomas Aquinas and the Natural Law Tradition*, ed. John Goyette, Mark S. Latkovic, and Richard S. Myers (Washington, DC: Catholic University of America Press, 2004), 136.

4. This is not to say, however, that accepting certain secular first principles is without danger. David Novak, for example, criticizes what he calls "radical secularity" as "regard[ing] the members of the society as having no religio-moral background at all." Novak supports a form of "moderate secularity," where religious adherents are required to explain how a "policy is for the good of any human society and not just the members of his or her traditional community." In contrast, radical secularism is rooted in a conception of individual autonomy that fails to acknowledge the role that

How else, then, might one understand the world? Interpreting another apocalyptic text, Stephen Robinson has argued that the great and abominable church in 1 Nephi 11–14 in the Book of Mormon refers primarily to hellenized Christianity.[5] While Robinson's interpretation is useful and interesting, as far as it goes, he never actually gives a direct account linking hellenized Christianity to the characteristics he finds associated with the great and abominable church in Nephi's vision (and the "Mother of Harlots" in the book of Revelation).[6] Moreover, even if readers were able to successfully link *historical* hellenized Christianity to the characteristics of Nephi's great and abominable church, a theological interpretation of the world in apocalyptic scriptural passages would require the additional interpretive step of identifying the beliefs, practices, and institutions in *modern* culture that best match the relevant characteristics of hellenized Christianity.

This last point is especially important. It is, in fact, altogether too easy to misunderstand both the original meaning and the modern significance of apocalyptic texts. The value of the ancient genre of apocalyptic texts, for the reading community who considers certain apocalyptic texts as canon, is its ability to have a powerful transforming effect *in the present.* Better, it is *in the process of interpretation*—especially in the most challenging and uncertain moments of interpretation—that the community becomes oriented by the kingdom of God rather than by the world. Although it may be possible to give a full-bodied historical interpretation of what apocalyptic texts have to say about the world, I will pursue a more theologically motivated

---

traditional values play in the exercise of moral agency and cultivation of desire for moral goods. David Novak, "Secularity without Secularism: The Best Political Position for Contemporary Jews," *Hedgehog Review* 8/1–2 (2006): 108–9.

5. Stephen E. Robinson, "Nephi's Great and Abominable Church," *Journal of Book of Mormon Studies* 7/1 (1998): 32–39. Hugh Nibley made a similar case earlier in *The World and the Prophets* (Salt Lake City: Deseret Book and FARMS, 1987).

6. Robinson lists five characteristics of the great and abominable church: (1) it is drunk with the blood of the Saints, (2) it seeks great wealth, (3) it is characterized by sexual immorality, (4) it has dominion over all the earth, and (5) it will be destroyed. It remains unclear exactly how each of these is to be directly linked to hellenized Christianity.

interpretation of what Nephi calls the great and abominable church. In light of our contemporary situation, I will identify the world with the unmitigated pursuit of power, especially as it can be obtained via wealth. My wager, in other words, is that the New Jerusalem envisioned by the text of Doctrine and Covenants 42 is best understood against the backdrop of our own situation: a world of beliefs, practices, and institutions that fosters a desire for power and wealth in a manner that fails to serve a legitimate higher good—such as caring for the poor.

Naturally, certain passages in LDS scripture might make one hesitate to jump too quickly on an interpretive bandwagon that, at first blush, offers a highly politicized, anticapitalist reading of section 42. A well-known example is Jacob's admonition in the Book of Mormon: "Before ye seek for riches, seek ye for the kingdom of God" (Jacob 2:18). Although this verse warns about seeking riches, it is often pointed out that there is no actual ban against seeking riches. And in fact, Jacob makes a startling promise in the next verse: "And after ye have obtained a hope in Christ ye shall obtain riches, if ye seek them; and ye will seek them for the intent to do good" (Jacob 2:19). Instead of giving an unrestrained condemnation of wealth, Jacob gives riches an explicitly articulated place in the life of a Christian disciple; nevertheless, Jacob clearly condemns improper pursuit of wealth. Any traditional LDS understanding of the world must account for Jacob's nuanced condemnation of the pursuit of riches.

The double temptation in a modern capitalist society to misinterpret Jacob's teachings regarding wealth—that is, as either completely approving or completely disapproving—mirrors the temptation to misinterpret the implications of apocalyptic metaphors regarding modern secular society. A careful reading of Doctrine and Covenants 42, one that is sensitive to textual, historical, and scriptural themes, reveals possibilities for *redeeming* the world—possibilities that are often missed. The purpose of the analysis that follows is to identify such possibilities. First, I will consider the boundary markers in D&C 42 between the world and the Zion community. I will then consider the textual and thematic links between the practice of consecration in D&C 42 and the Holy War ban in ancient Israel. Finally, I will apply all these insights to the question of caring for the poor.

Community boundaries

In early church history, Doctrine and Covenants 42 was referred to as "The Laws of the Church of Christ," or the Law, and it served in a crucial way to draw out the nature of the boundary between God's people and the world. As is increasingly recognized, the law functioned in a similar way among ancient Israelites as a community marker that distinguished Israelites from their non-Israelite neighbors. Moreover, apocalyptic texts are also concerned with a differentiating boundary between God's community and the world in which God's community lives. In light of these boundary-marking roles consistently played by God's word, it is interesting to note the clearly apocalyptic resonance that the term New Jerusalem has in LDS scripture. Interestingly, prior to the restoration, the word pair New Jerusalem was found in scripture only in the book of Revelation. In restoration scripture, however, New Jerusalem occurs seventeen times: eight in the Book of Mormon (only in the books of 3 Nephi and Ether), once in the Book of Moses, and eight times in the Doctrine and Covenants—with half of these last eight occurrences in section 42 (vv. 9, 35, 62, and 67). The apocalyptic focus of D&C 42 is already clear from these details alone.

When Joseph Smith received the Law, the Second Great Awakening was well underway, a movement infused with the language and ethos of apocalypticism. In an overview of the history and scholarly literature pertaining to American apocalypticism, Stephen Stein suggests, "The most useful categories for dealing with apocalypticism in the American historical experience are 'religious apocalypticism' and 'secular apocalypticism.'" The key distinction, for Stein, is as follows: "The former involves in some fashion the quest for salvation, righteousness or wisdom, however defined; the latter is by definition limited to temporal goals reflected in society, politics, or aesthetics."[7] Although this distinction is helpful for understanding various religious and

---

7. The influential ideas of Jonathan Edwards were rooted in what Stein describes as "a tradition of apocalyptic exegesis that had existed for centuries within Christianity . . . [particularly] beholden to hermeneutical patterns within the Anglo-American Puritan tradition." See Stephen Stein, "American Millennial Visions: Towards a Construction of a New Architectonic of American Apocalypticism," in *Imagining the End: Visions of*

social movements in American history, it is not as obviously helpful for understanding Mormon apocalypticism. After all, the spiritual and the temporal are so deeply interfused in LDS theology that it is difficult to draw a sharp distinction between religious and spiritual or secular and temporal implications.[8] There is, nevertheless, a *negative* sense in which this distinction can be applied to the church's history. If apocalypticism is understood as simply "defensive against" or distinctly "pure from" modern, secular institutions, then this risks a mistaken, overly *fundamentalist* understanding of Mormonism; if, on the other hand, apocalypticism is understood as merely "relevant to" the world, in a strictly accommodating manner, then this risks a mistaken, overly syncretic, overly *secular* understanding of LDS beliefs.[9]

If the spiritual and the temporal in Mormonism are bound together so that one cannot be understood without the other, it is nevertheless important to understand the hierarchical nature of the relationship of the spiritual and the temporal. In line with Jacob's words quoted above, claiming that an "intent to do good" must govern any seeking for riches, LDS theology requires the spiritual to orient the temporal, rather than vice versa. And this relationship is always precarious. Temporal concerns can debase and crowd out spirituality; spiritual concerns can be misconstrued in overly mystical or fundamentalist ways that have no temporal relevance. This ongoing tension is reflected in human society by means of competing beliefs, practices, and institutions that orient individuals and communities toward different ends. Such ends include greater economic efficiency, power, or wealth on the one hand, but greater compassion, honesty, or equality on the other.

An important function of scriptural texts—and apocalyptic texts in particular—is to bring this tension between the world and the religious community to light in a transformative way. The transformative

---

Apocalypse from the Ancient Middle East to Modern America, ed. Abbas Amanat and Magnus Bernhardsson (New York: I. B. Tauris, 2002), 188, 211.

8. See Terryl L. Givens, *People of Paradox: A History of Mormon Culture* (New York: Oxford University Press, 2007), 37–52.

9. These phrases in quotation marks come from a discussion of these themes in James Davison Hunter, *To Change the World: The Irony Tragedy, and Possibility of Christianity in the Late Modern World* (New York: Oxford University Press, 2010), 223.

potential of scriptural texts is realized in the act of reading, especially when the community is required to interpret tensive, multivalent symbols.[10] Christian theologian Ellen Charry, in the context of persecution themes, suggests that the ambiguity of apocalyptic writing can produce a "search for the truth" that is common to both the persecuted and the persecutor.[11] This kind of transformative ambiguity is a crucial—not merely an accidental—characteristic of apocalyptic writing. Leonard Thompson also argues that ambiguous symbols and "soft boundaries" lead, ideally, to processes of interpretation that are transformative. In a description that surprisingly resonates with Latter-day Saints, Thompson writes:

> [In the book of Revelation] there is no spatial or temporal dualism between the kingdom of the world and the

---

10. The language of tensive symbols with polyvalent meanings, as opposed to steno symbols with univalent meaning, is discussed in Philip Wheelwright, *Metaphor and Reality* (Bloomington: Indiana University Press, 1962). In a similar vein, Stephen Cook writes, "The worldview of millennial groups combines a linear view of history with a futuristic eschatology that pictures an imminent radical change in the way things are." Cook, *Prophecy and Apocalypticism: The Postexilic Social Setting* (Minneapolis: Fortress, 1995), 26. For a discussion of the various ways in which apocalyptic texts have captured the imagination of various communities in history, see Wes Howard-Brook and Anthony Gwyther, *Unveiling Empire: Reading Revelation Then and Now* (Maryknoll, NY: Orbis Books, 1999), 1–45. From an LDS perspective, James Faulconer writes, "Apocalyptic theology ... is defined by what it does rather than by its objects and methods." Faulconer, "Rethinking Theology," 117. Reflecting on Isaiah 55, I also discuss the transformative potential of scriptural texts in Robert B. Couch, "'Without Money': Equality and the Transformative Power of God's Word," in *Perspectives on Mormon Theology: Scriptural Theology*, ed. James E. Faulconer and Joseph M. Spencer (Salt Lake City: Greg Kofford Books, 2015), 31–56.

11. Ellen T. Charry writes, "Daniel and John integrate two elements that display the ambiguity of apocalyptic and bring them to bear on the interpretation of the suffering of God's people. First, self-examination is required, even on the part of those being persecuted. Second, God's rescue of the faithful is cause for self-examination among those who have persecuted. Thus, victim and oppressor are joined together in a common search for the truth about themselves and about God who is in the midst of their struggle." Charry, "'A Sharp Two-Edged Sword': Pastoral Implications of Apocalyptic," in *Character and Scripture: Moral Formation, Community, and Biblical Interpretation*, ed. William P. Brown (Grand Rapids, MI: Eerdmans, 2002), 352–53.

kingdom of God. God creates and sustains all things. Transformations and changes permeate every boundary and break down every distinction because there is an underlying dynamic system into and out of which all distinctions fold and unfold.... This monistic flow of divinely ordered being can never quite be compartmentalized into creature and creator, God and Satan, this age and the age to come, or heaven and earth. That is the unbroken world disclosed through the language of the Apocalypse.... Revelation discloses in its depth or innerness a wholeness of vision consonant with the intertexture found at the surface level of his language. At all levels, signifiers, signifieds, deep structures, and surface structures form homologies, not contradictory oppositions. The logic of the vision does not progress from oppositions to their resolution. Rather, in all its aspects the language speaks from unbroken wholeness to unbroken wholeness.[12]

From a Latter-day Saint perspective, Thompson's understanding of the homologous nature of the book of Revelation, with its "not contradictory oppositions," has important resonance with Lehi's teaching about opposition (see 2 Nephi 2:11). Lehi says that oppositions not only exist, but they exist *in all things*. To think otherwise is to misunderstand the nature of the world and the plan of salvation that God initiated. To recognize this always-present, noncontradictory opposition is to recognize the importance of agency—the always-present possibility of sin on the one hand and repentance on the other. At a more communal level, the implication of an always-present, noncontradictory opposition underscores the ongoing danger of sin among those in the covenant community and the ongoing possibility of repentance among those in worldly society. To understand Doctrine and Covenants 42, it is important to keep in mind this ever-present battle between the

---

12. Leonard L. Thompson, *The Book of Revelation: Apocalypse and Empire* (New York: Oxford University Press, 1990), 90.

world and the New Jerusalem, and the porous boundary that marks their separation.

This porous boundary marking the opposition between the New Jerusalem and the world is on display in Doctrine and Covenants 42 by the repeated use of the phrase "shall be cast out." The uniqueness of this phrase manifests itself when other scriptural passages that enumerate second-tablet commandments are compared to D&C 42. Regardless of whether the "shall be cast out" phrase has *intentional* structural significance, it is nevertheless interesting to see what emerges when the structural occurrences of this unique, boundary-marking phrase are analyzed. Doing so reveals two points worth noting.

First, the phrase "shall be cast out" occurs six times in verses 20–28 and then again a seventh time in verse 37 after a digression regarding matters of economics, consecration, and the poor.[13] From an apocalyptic perspective, this delay between the sixth and seventh occurrences is reminiscent of the delay between the sixth and seventh seals in Revelation 7:1–17 and the sixth and seventh trumpet blasts in Revelation 10:1–11:13. According to at least one biblical exegete, the purpose of this delay between the sixth and seventh trumpet blasts, with its accompanying numerical reversal, is to "bring the nations to repentance of idolatry and conversion to the true God."[14] A similar invitation to repent, extended to the nations, can be seen at work in Doctrine and Covenants 42, particularly in the historical changes made between the 1833 and 1835 renderings of the text. In the 1833 version, what is now verse 39 reads, "For it shall come to pass that which I spake by the mouth of my prophets shall be fulfilled for I will consecrate the riches of the Gentiles unto my people which are of the house of Israel." Early

---

13. An eighth occurrence in the section occurs in verse 75, but that verse is perhaps best considered as a separate textual unit, following Grant Underwood's approach in "'The Laws of the Church of Christ' (D&C 42): A Textual and Historical Analysis," in *The Doctrine and Covenants: Revelations in Context*, ed. Andrew H. Hedges, J. Spencer Fluhman, and Alonzo L. Gaskill (Provo, UT: BYU Religious Studies Center and Deseret Book, 2008), 108–41.

14. Richard Bauckham, "Revelation," in *The Oxford Bible Commentary*, ed. John Barton and John Muddiman (New York: Oxford University Press, 2001), 1296. The nine-tenths spared in the book of Revelation contrasts in a surprising way with the usual one-tenth spared (cf. Isaiah 6:13; Amos 5:3; 1 Kings 19:18).

Latter-day Saints understood this verse to mean that righteous members would obtain the riches of the wicked gentiles, an attitude that was used to justify retaliations against their enemies.[15] However, Joseph Smith changed the wording of verse 39 for the 1835 edition to the following (changes appear in italics): "For I will consecrate *of* the riches of *those who embrace my gospel among* the Gentiles, unto *the poor of* my people *who* are of the house of Israel." These changes (coupled with similar changes in verses 30, 37, and 38) cast the gentiles/nations in an explicitly redemptive role, rather than the more antagonistic role conveyed by the earlier text.[16]

Second, if the "shall be cast out" phrase is considered in terms of thematic development, the following chiastic structure can be discerned:

A   Property: "Thou shalt not steal; and he that stealeth and will not repent *shall be cast out*" (v. 20).

    B   Language: "Thou shalt not lie; he that lieth and will not repent *shall be cast out*" (v. 21).

       C   Chastity: "Thou shalt love thy wife with all thy heart, and shalt cleave unto her and none else. And he that looketh upon a woman to lust after her shall deny the faith, and shall not have the Spirit; and if he repents not he *shall be cast out*. Thou shalt not commit adultery; and he that committeth adultery, and repenteth not, *shall be cast out*. But he that has committed adultery and repents with all his heart, and forsaketh it, and doeth it no more, thou shalt forgive; But if he doeth it again, he shall not be forgiven, but *shall be cast out*" (vv. 22–26).

---

15. For more on the historical context of these textual changes, see Underwood, "'Laws of the Church of Christ,'" 108–41. The historical situation could also be understood as a juncture between the two different paths represented by the more violent and antagonist text of 1 Maccabees compared to the more peaceful apocalyptic visions recorded in Daniel, Revelation, and other Old Testament prophetic texts. For more on the peaceful nature of the apocalyptic texts canonized in the Bible, see Howard-Brook and Gwyther, *Unveiling Empire*, 46–86, 136–56.

16. Underwood, "'Laws of the Church of Christ,'" 108–41.

    B′   Language: "Thou shalt not speak evil of thy neighbor, nor do him any harm. Thou knowest my laws concerning these things are given in my scriptures; he that sinneth and repenteth not *shall be cast out*" (vv. 27–28).

A′   Property: "And it shall come to pass, that he that sinneth and repenteth not *shall be cast out* of the church, and shall not receive again that which he has consecrated unto the poor and the needy of my church, or in other words, unto me" (v. 37).

When the text is arranged in this way, a thematic movement can be discerned from the most mundane, "object"-based concept of property in the beginning and ending chiastic units to the most sacred, relation-based concept of chastity at the central chiastic unit, passing along the way by the intermediate case of language. Also, the second occurrence of each chiastic unit can be understood as giving the concepts in the first half a "higher" inflection: the place of lust in the first half of the chiastic unit is replaced by forgiveness to the repentant adulterer in the second half; the injunction against lying in the first half is replaced by an injunction against speaking evil of one's neighbor; the prohibition on stealing in the first half is replaced by the concept of consecration in the second. Accordingly, property is first conceived in these verses merely as a temporal object that can be stolen—and thus idolatrously desired and individually grasped—but later becomes spiritually inflected as something that can be offered as a sacred gift to the poor. This transformation of property from a worldly object to a sacred gift typifies the redemptive, transformative possibilities made manifest in apocalyptic texts.

In considering the context of the Doctrine and Covenants as a whole, the phrase "cast out" occurs sixteen times in the current edition. Most of these usages draw a holy-unholy boundary where the casting out can be understood as a consequence of transgressive action.[17]

---

17. Eight of these occurrences are in Doctrine and Covenants 42, already discussed. A ninth occurrence is in section 41, which anticipates the use and meaning of the phrase in section 42. Three others appear in the context of casting out devils (D&C 35:9; 84:67; 124:98). In another occurrence, D&C 101:1–2 reads, "Concerning your brethren who have been afflicted, and persecuted, and cast out from the land of their inheritance—

This larger context underscores the function that D&C 42 plays in the establishment of a new community—one again based on stark differences (relative to the world) but with porous boundaries. Implicit in the community envisaged by section 42 and its associated scriptural resonances is what might be called a conditional tolerance for sin, where the condition of possibility for this tolerance is repentance. Repentance mediates the oppositional boundary between the world and the covenant community. Inasmuch as repentance is a real possibility that can be hoped for, redemption within the world is possible. Secular society, inasmuch as it tolerates religious communities, seems to be redeemable in this important sense. Also in this sense, as I hope now to show, secular society can be usefully contrasted with the conditions under which the ancient Israelite practice of the Holy War ban arose.

Consecration and the Holy War ban

The term *consecration*, as used in modern restoration scripture, has linguistic ties to the Hebrew term *cherem*, which is used in the Old Testament to refer to the Holy War ban. Exploration of this linguistic tie can be further motivated by first considering the use of the term *consecration* in modern restoration scripture.

Consecration is used seven times in the current edition of Doctrine and Covenants 42, whereas the term appears only three times in the

---

I, the Lord, have suffered the affliction to come upon them ... in consequence of their transgressions." In D&C 101:40, the imagery of salt that has lost its savor is said to be "good for nothing only to be cast out and trodden under the feet of men" (cf. D&C 103:10), an expression taken directly from Matthew 5:13 and used in 3 Nephi 12:13 and 16:15. One other occurrence is in D&C 29:41 with reference to Adam being "cast out" of the Garden of Eden. The thick Mormon conception of the plan of salvation—including a premortal life, agency, judgment, and resurrection—can be more tightly connected to the "cast out" phrase by considering two other scriptural chapters where the phrase "cast out" occurs: First, in the Book of Mormon, Alma describes how the wicked will be "cast out" of God's presence "because of their own iniquity" (Alma 40:13) and "consigned to partake of the fruits of their labors or their works, which have been evil" (Alma 40:26). Second, in Revelation 12:9, "the great dragon was cast out, that old serpent, called the Devil, and Satan, which deceiveth the whole world: he was cast out into the earth, and his angels were cast out with him."

1833 Book of Commandments version of the text.[18] The four additional occurrences appear in the revised text in verses 32–33. In the original text of what is now verse 30, members are required to consecrate all their property: "Thou shalt consecrate *all* thy properties, that which thou hast unto me, with a covenant and deed" (emphasis added). This was changed in the 1835 edition to read, "Thou wilt remember the poor, and consecrate *of* thy properties" (emphasis added). As noted by Michael Marquardt, "The altered portion weakened the requirement … leaving the percentage—all or part—ambiguous. In fact, it seemed to imply that the amount might be a matter of personal preference."[19] A key difference between the 1833 "all" and the 1835 "of" version of D&C 42 is the mediating role the church plays between individual members of the community and the larger context of worldly society.[20] This difference should not be understood as a simple lessening of what is required by the Law.[21] Rather, the textual change makes the relationship between the individual and the poor more immediate and less regulated by the institutional structures of the church. By reducing the institutional claim on the individual, the text grants the individual a larger extrainstitutional presence in—and engagement with—worldly society.

---

18. For a detailed account of the changes, see Underwood, "'Laws of the Church of Christ,'" 108–41, and H. Michael Marquardt, *The Joseph Smith Revelations: Text and Commentary* (Salt Lake City: Signature Books, 1999), 107–15.

19. Marquardt, *Joseph Smith Revelations*, 114.

20. For a more in-depth theological treatment of this change, see Joseph M. Spencer, *For Zion: A Mormon Theology of Hope* (Salt Lake City: Greg Kofford Books, 2014), especially 107–46.

21. President Gordon B. Hinckley has affirmed that "the law of consecration [was] not done away with and [is] still in effect." Gordon B. Hinckley, *Teachings of Gordon B. Hinckley* (Salt Lake City: Deseret Book, 1997), 639. See also Steven C. Harper, "'All Things Are the Lord's': The Law of Consecration in the Doctrine and Covenants," in *Doctrine and Covenants: Revelations in Context*, 212–28. President Ezra Taft Benson gave a modern definition of the covenant associated with consecration: "that we consecrate our time, talents, strength, property, and money for the upbuilding of the kingdom of God on this earth and the establishment of Zion." Ezra Taft Benson, *Teachings of Ezra Taft Benson* (Salt Lake City: Bookcraft, 1998), 121.

Doctrine and Covenants 42:39 reads, "For I will *consecrate of the riches* of those who embrace my gospel among the Gentiles unto the poor of my people who are of the house of Israel" (emphasis added). This verse bears close resemblance to Micah 4:13, which is also quoted by Christ in 3 Nephi 20:19. In the King James Version of the Bible, this reads: "I will *consecrate their gain* unto the Lord, and their substance unto the Lord of the whole earth" (emphasis added).[22] The Hebrew term translated here as "consecrate" is *cherem*. Although other Hebrew terms in the King James Version are more frequently translated as "consecrate" in English, the word *cherem* is worth considering quite carefully—not only because of the similar phrasing in Micah and the repeated use of this phrase in the Book of Mormon, but also because the term *cherem* has interesting theological import pertaining specifically to the question of community-society boundaries.

The term *cherem* is most frequently translated by the King James Version as "destroy." At first glance, the terms *consecrate* and *destroy* seem more like antonyms than synonyms, so it is surprising they are used to translate the same Hebrew term. However, the connection between these terms can be understood by exploring the nature of Holy War and the associated practice of the Holy War ban in the Old Testament.[23] For example, the three consecutive chapters in Joshua 6–8 prominently feature the topic of Holy War. Chapters 6 and 8 contain positive stories, where the rules of the Holy War ban—laid out in Deuteronomy 20:10–18 and Joshua 6:17–19—are properly followed. As a consequence of this obedience, Israel successfully takes the city

---

22. Grant Underwood suggests that the scriptural allusion here is to Isaiah 61:6, and he explores the significance of this passage in Mormon history. Interestingly, 2 Nephi 2:2 and 2 Nephi 33:4 also use language of God "consecrating" something (afflictions and prayers, respectively) for "gain."

23. Note that the context of both Micah's and Christ's prophecies are related to Holy War imagery. In the context of Micah's apocalyptic prophecy, the nations have gathered together in order to destroy Jerusalem (Micah 4:11), but the Lord, who has arranged this, effects a reversal of what the nations expect, so that Israel ends up thrashing the nations. In the context of Christ's prophecy among the Nephites, Christ is specifically prophesying that a remnant of the house of Jacob will go forth among the gentiles and destroy those who have hardened their hearts against the fullness of the gospel (see 3 Nephi 20:27).

of Jericho and conquers the Canaanites.[24] The Holy War ban required that all captured animals and humans be put to death, and that all wealth be *consecrated* by being put into a sanctuary for God. As the Old Testament theologian Gordon McConville explains, the joint rationale for these practices "derives from 'holiness' ideas; in animal sacrifice, the animal is regarded as having become 'holy' in a technical sense. Similarly, the slaughter of a city's population in Holy War is a kind of sacrifice to God. Further, since it is seen in this way, it is not optional but an absolute obligation."[25] Although the similarity in logic thus expressed between Holy War and sacrifice is a common interpretation, I will make a different argument below.

Joshua 7 contains the negative story of a man who violates the Holy War ban and causes the Israelite armies to be defeated. When this man, Achan, is discovered to be the culprit who violated the ban, he offers the following explanation of his behavior: "When I saw among the spoils a goodly Babylonish garment, and two hundred shekels of silver, and a wedge of gold of fifty shekels weight, then I coveted them, and took them; and, behold, they are hid in the earth in the midst of my tent, and the silver under it" (Joshua 7:21). Money and the economically valuable ("goodly") garment play a central thematic role in this passage and comprise the central motive for Achan's disobedience of the Holy War ban. The Hebrew term translated "covet" in this verse is *chamad*, which is the same word used in the second tablet's injunction against coveting (see Exodus 20:17). Although the term *covet* does not occur in Doctrine and Covenants 42, three of the seven "cast out" phrases occur during the discussion of adultery; moreover, in Christian society—especially in America during the 1830s—adultery is understood as being closely related to covetousness, partly because of the connection made in the Sermon the Mount (Matthew 5:27–28).[26]

---

24. Given the discussion above regarding the possible significance of seven occurrences of the phrase "cast out" in section 42, it is interesting to note how the number seven also plays a significant role in the account here, including what might be construed as a delay in the narrative between the sixth and seventh days of marching in Joshua 6:15–19.

25. Gordon McConville, "Joshua," in *Oxford Bible Commentary*, 164.

26. The term translated "lust" in the KJV version of Matthew 5:28 is the same Greek word *epithymeō* translated in the LXX as "covet" in, for example, Exodus 20:17.

Achan's violation of the Holy War ban uncomfortably entails consequences for his entire family, and this detail has major implications for how the Holy War ban should be understood. Philip Stern argues that "the biblical conception of collective responsibility illustrated by Numbers 16:20–22" governs the destruction of Achan's family, but this stands *in contrast* to sacrificial motifs, since "the family of a malpracticing sacrifice was never punished."[27] As previously noted, scholars have generally proposed an understanding of the Holy War ban that is similar to the concept of sacrifice. Stern, however, argues that "to apply the term *sacrifice* to the war ban is to mischaracterize it profoundly" and, moreover, that "mass killing in battle was never viewed as sacrifice in the ancient Near East—not in Egypt, not in Assyria, not among the Hittites."[28] Besides sacrifice having more individualistic connotations, Stern argues that the consecration-based logic of the Holy War ban is rooted more deeply in a concept of exchange.[29] This interpretation is surprising since one natural understanding of the distinction between sacrifice and consecration is the exact opposite of Stern's. Whereas sacrifice entails giving up something good *in exchange* for something

---

27. Philip D. Stern, "Isaiah 34, Chaos, and the Ban," in *Ki Baruch Hu: Ancient Near Eastern, Biblical, and Judaic Studies in Honor of Baruch A. Levine*, ed. Robert Chazan, William W. Hallo, and Lawrence H. Schiffman (Winona Lake, IN: Eisenbrauns, 1999), 394. Regarding the punishment of Achan's family, Trent Butler acknowledges that Achan's punishment "is now interpreted as meaning [destruction of] his family and possessions." Butler, *Joshua* (Dallas: Thomas Nelson, 1983), 86. Susan Niditch explains, "The shocking list of that which is to be annihilated includes Achan, what he has stolen, his sons and daughters, oxen, donkeys, sheep, and all he had (Josh 7:24). The text veers from singular to plural in vv. 25–26 in referring to those who are killed, a scribal oscillation perhaps stemming from discomfort with the totality of the destruction, but it is clear that at least one tradition, the one that links up best with v. 24, imagines Achan and all that belongs to him burned with fire and stoned." Niditch, *War in the Hebrew Bible: A Study in the Ethics of Violence* (New York: Oxford University Press, 1993), 59.
28. Stern, "Isaiah 34, Chaos, and the Ban," 395.
29. "The war ban is also an exchange in a way a sacrifice normally is not.... In contrast to sacrifice, in which nothing is guaranteed in return, in the war ban, God always assures the victory! There is no instance of the use of ban terminology when Israel ... lost to the foe, in contrast to the sacrifice in which the outcome was uncertain or in which the sacrifice was simply an act of piety." Stern, "Isaiah 34, Chaos, and the Ban," 392.

better, consecration requires a more selfless attitude where what is given up is *not* linked to hopes of getting something in return. Stern's claim, however, hinges on the concept of a guarantee. What makes the Holy War ban a stricter mode of exchange than sacrifice is the stronger and more precise guarantee that adherence to the Holy War ban implies. With sacrifice, it is easy to doubt the sufficiency of the sacrifice and the possibility that it will be rewarded. With the Holy War ban, however, this kind of doubt vanishes: if the requirements of the ban are fulfilled, then victory is the sure reward.[30]

The sure nature of the Holy War guarantee can be understood, in LDS terms, in the context of an eternal covenant and the whole-hearted, other-abiding nature in which covenants are made. The problem with the logic of sacrifice, at least as typically conceived, is that desires do not necessarily change (see more on this below in the context of caring for the poor). One who hopes for something in return for a sacrifice can remain under a certain economic cast of mind. Under the logic of consecration, however, all preconceived personal agendas are given up in kenotic fashion in a genuine willingness to do whatever is asked. When consecration occurs, a true change of heart also occurs. Only this kind of consecrated way of relating can guarantee a fullness of spiritual blessings.

To better understand the scriptural linkages between covetousness, consecration, desire, and community, the Apostle Paul's discussion in Romans 7:7–13 is worth consideration. James Dunn argues that Paul's discussion of lust and covetousness is a "semi-allegorical reading of Genesis 2–3 . . . [where the] command not to eat of the tree of the knowledge of good and evil (Gen 2.17) is read as a particular expression of the commandment, 'You shall not covet.'" Dunn goes on to suggest that in Romans 7, Paul may have been "deliberately meshing in the

---

30. In modern scripture, a similar logic of "guarantee" can be found where guaranteed blessings follow whole-hearted obedience. For example, Doctrine and Covenants 121:45 reads, "Let thy bowels also be full of charity towards all men, . . . and let virtue garnish thy thoughts unceasingly; then shall thy confidence wax strong in the presence of God." Here, the guarantee of confidence is contingent upon a description of a heart and mind that invokes phrases suggesting full consecration: "*full* of charity"; "towards *all* men"; "let virtue garnish thy thoughts *unceasingly.*"

story of Israel ... [who] experienced sin provoking covetousness by means of the commandment given on Mount Sinai," a sin that is reminiscent of a link between idolatry and slaughter.[31] Dunn's reading of Paul gives precedent in Christian scripture for understanding desire as a central concept of community and violence that links the first story in the Old Testament with Israel's subsequent historical memory and relationship with God—a relationship in constant turmoil because of Israel's idolatrous desires. Against this scriptural background, the emphasis and linkage in Doctrine and Covenants 42 between the themes of covetousness/adultery and idolatry/consecration manifests the importance of protecting the covenant community against the incursion of unrighteous worldly desires.

In Old Testament history, sacrificial practices were not particularly successful at staving off idolatrous desires. Condemnation of impure desires associated with ritual sacrifice is a common theme in the writings of the latter prophets, the Psalms, the Gospel of Mark, and, most importantly—because of its intersection with the theme of the Holy War ban—1 Samuel 15.[32] On Meir Sternberg's reading of 1 Samuel 15, the command given to Saul to smite Amalek begins in verses 1–3 with textual references to the repeated wrongs previously committed by the Amalekites in order to "eliminate all traces of arbitrariness from the divine command but also evoke a long and eventful history of one-sided aggression."[33] The text then goes on to offer an elaborate account of Samuel posing a series of questions to Saul, whose responses establish an incriminating case for his failure to adhere to the conditions of the Holy War ban. Sternberg argues that the purpose of this elaborate story is to help the reader learn that Saul is in fact guilty and that Saul refuses to take advantage of the repeated opportunities Samuel presents for him to confess and repent of his misdeeds.[34]

---

31. See a full explanation of Romans 7:7–13 in James D. G. Dunn, *The Theology of Paul the Apostle* (Grand Rapids, MI: Eerdmans, 1997), 99–101.

32. See Isaiah 1:10–11, 13; Jeremiah 7:21–26; Hosea 6:6; Amos 5:21–24; Micah 6:6–8; Psalms 40:6–8; 50:9; 51:16; and Mark 12:33.

33. Meir Sternberg, *The Poetics of Biblical Narrative: Ideological Literature and the Drama of Reading* (Indianapolis: Indiana University Press, 1987), 486.

34. Regarding Saul's part in the dialogue, Sternberg writes, "As far as concerns the aims of the tale ... the vital part of the dialogue centers on the speeches made by Saul,

Switching to Samuel's part in the dialogue, Sternberg argues that, acting as God's agent, Samuel suggests that Saul's fate is not predetermined, but "indeterminate, contingent on moral choice."[35] The narrative, after all, begins with God repenting of the fact that he has "set up Saul to be King" (1 Samuel 15:11). Moreover, the emphasis is on Saul's "past misdeed ('he has turned back from following me') and [God's] present emotion ('I repent') more than the future scenario typical of a forecast. And the sense of an *open* future gains further support from the built-in reminder that God is quite capable of changing his mind with the change of circumstance. Having started by repenting, he may well finish by repenting this repentance."[36] According to Sternberg's reading, then, Samuel's prolonged discussion with Saul not only provides the latter with repeated opportunities to make an immediate confession—like Achan in the past, Jonathan in Saul's present, and David in a future generation, each of whom "promptly confesses his sins once charged"[37]—but it also has the effect of drawing the reader in, inviting the reader to participate in a moral evaluation of Saul's behavior. The biblical narrator is, in effect, inviting the reader to participate in the narrative and therefore to repent. This invitation has the potential of effecting a disruption and transformation of time and place inhabited by the reader. This invitation also has the potential of disrupting the reader's actual, present desires, including the desire to be obedient to God's commandments. Obedience, after all, is what Samuel tells Saul is called for, not mere sacrifice. In this sense, the story of Saul has the potential to change the reader's attitude toward his or her own religious actions. Thus, readers may gain a genuine desire to listen and obey in a wholehearted, consecrated way, rather than in a double-minded, superficial manner focused on achieving an extrinsic reward.[38]

---

who is meant to condemn himself by his incessant shifts and turns. And this structure of repetition makes excellent sense in dramatic (psychological, situational) as well as rhetorical terms: Saul has every reason to conceal or whitewash his sin, and he retreats only step by step, version by defensive version." Sternberg, *Poetics of Biblical Narrative*, 501.

35. Sternberg, *Poetics of Biblical Narrative*, 502.

36. Sternberg, *Poetics of Biblical Narrative*, 502.

37. Sternberg, *Poetics of Biblical Narrative*, 509.

38. Regarding double-mindedness, see Søren Kierkegaard, *Purity of Heart Is to Will One Thing*, trans. Douglas V. Steere (San Francisco: HarperOne, 1956).

Through the concept of the Holy War ban and the term *cherem*, the ancient Israelite theological struggle to preserve its communal identity amid a worldly society is linked to the concept of consecration presented in Doctrine and Covenants 42. In both cases, the practice of consecration cannot be properly understood merely as a sacrificial act; rather, it requires a transformation of desire. The call of ancient and modern scriptural texts requires readers in the community to recognize the tension between the ends pursued by the covenant community and those pursued by the world. Worldly desire is scripturally typified in the context of the Holy War ban by the avarice displayed by Achan and the self-deceptive, merely sacrificial obedience exhibited by Saul.

Care for the poor

After a discussion of community-marking, second-tablet commandments, Doctrine and Covenants 42 moves to the economically inflected themes of consecration and the poor. As discussed above, the term *consecration* is usefully understood against a scriptural background in which God repeatedly attempts to purify the avaricious desires of his covenant community. To understand these concepts as they might function and resonate in modern society, it is useful to contrast the way that poverty is understood and discussed in modern, secular society with the way that LDS scripture conceives of the problem of caring for the poor. This is not to say that the two conceptions are inimical to each other, but that the scriptural conception offers an important and useful spiritual supplement to purely temporal, secular conceptions.

In the original version of the revelation, an injunction to remember the poor was present; however, in that version, the term *poor* actually occurred only once in what is now verse 34: "the residue shall be kept in my storehouse, to administer to the poor and needy." In 1835, the term *poor* was added several times, for a total of six occurrences, a change preserved in the current edition of the Doctrine and Covenants. At first blush, these changes might be viewed as having no particular theological significance, since they reflect practical and legal expediencies from the time. Grant Underwood, for example, argues as follows: "Because charitable donations were legally safeguarded in a way that communal resource sharing was not, in several places in the Law, wording was added to similarly clarify that the poor were the specific beneficiaries of consecrations."[39] But even if legal pressures fully explain the wording changes, this does not imply that the changes are not also theologically important.

There are at least two reasons to think these textual changes were theologically significant. First, a similar emphasis on the poor around the same time characterized Joseph Smith's work on the New Translation of Genesis, where Melchizedek is described as "the high priest, and the keeper of the storehouse of God; Him whom God had appointed to receive tithes for the poor" (Genesis 14:37–38 JST).[40] This change in a tangential scriptural text is poorly explained simply by legal pressures of the 1830s. Second, the institutional action taken by the church itself to accommodate the legal particularities of the time requires theological explanation. The fluctuating tension between the early Mormon community and the US government could have been handled in a different, perhaps more confrontational way. Understanding why the church took this accommodating course of action, in the face of legal circumstances and political pressures, has important implications for understanding political and religious boundaries today—questions that, in turn, have important implications for understanding the role of the poor in section 42.

To reach a modern, apocalyptically inflected understanding of the poor, it is important to recognize that in ancient contexts, secular space did not exist in the way it does today. The separation of church and state is, for the most part, a modern concept. Wes Howard-Brook and Anthony Gwyther write,

---

39. Underwood, "'Laws of the Church of Christ,'" 120. For more discussion regarding the historical pressures and the changes made to subsequent sections of the Doctrine and Covenants, see Christopher C. Smith, "The Inspired Fictionalization of the 1835 United Firm Revelations," *Claremont Journal of Mormon Studies* 1/1 (April 2011): 15–31.

40. The New Translation is in fact referenced in Doctrine and Covenants 42:56. See Underwood, "'Laws of the Church of Christ,'" 125. Interestingly, Genesis 14 also touches on themes regarding the Holy War ban, *avant la lettre*.

> [The book of] Revelation casts a critical eye on Rome's economic exploitation, its politics of seduction, its violence, and its imperial hubris or arrogance. To oppose the Roman Empire necessarily involved a rejection of the spirituality that helped the empire run like a well-oiled machine. Yet the rejection of that spirituality, manifest in the imperial cult, was part of a total rejection of the empire. This is a consequence of the inseparability of religion and politics in antiquity.[41]

Howard-Brook and Gwyther go on to argue that applying the meaning of Revelation to a modern context requires that readers understand today's empire as global capitalism, a recognition further suggesting that the faithful must engage in some form of political resistance to capitalism.

On the one hand, there is something very right about this interpretation, especially in the way that it captures various despiritualizing tendencies arising from forces of social and political—but especially *economic*—globalization.[42] On the other hand, this politicized approach

---

41. Howard-Brook and Gwyther, *Unveiling Empire*, 116.

42. The phenomenon of globalization can be understood in political, economic, and social terms: "In the political field the term refers to the increasing role of international governmental and nongovernmental organizations in organizing access to rights, identities, and material benefits; in the economic field to the increasing role of multinational corporations, and the interlocking of global financial institutions; and in the social field to changes in the volume and types of immigration and cultural flows." The phenomenon of *neoliberal* globalization can be understood in terms of "the new power of owners of large, multinational corporations that benefit from economic policies associated with innovation, trade liberalization, reduced government spending on entitlements and decreased state restrictions on labor, health, and environmental hazards of production.... The term 'neoliberalism' is used here to describe ideologies and practices that have also varied widely over time and across countries but have a family resemblance on three issues: a tendency to prefer markets over governments as instruments of policy (via privatization or, where regulatory policies are deemed necessary, via regulatory interventions that use marketplace mechanisms such as cap-and-trade systems); to favor trade liberalization over protectionism (with reductions in tariffs, subsidies, floating currencies, and regional and global trade agreements); and to approach poverty from the vantage point of self-responsibility, decentralized public-private partnerships,

to understanding the "total rejection of the empire" in apocalyptic texts risks obscuring the boundaries between church and state as they exist in modern, secular societies. One way to justify resistance to an overly politicized understanding of the message contained in scripture (especially apocalyptic) is to consider Jesus's response to the question about whether it is lawful to pay tribute to Caesar: "Render therefore unto Caesar the things which are Caesar's" (Matthew 22:21). Jesus's response can be understood as a recognition of the protosecular, limited scope of the Roman empire at the time and the possibility of living simultaneously according to both the dictates of God's kingdom and the limited demands of political economy at the time.[43] This teaching, in a sense, represents the culminating repudiation of the practice of Holy War, which was only necessary during less secular times: whereas previous generations had viewed foreign cultures as *anathema* (literally, since this is the ancient Greek translation of *cherem*), times had changed, and relatively peaceful coexistence by the time of Christ was a real

---

enterprise development, and other orientations to economic development expected to produce overall increases in the standard of living rather than redistributive change." Both of these definitional quotes come from Kelly Moore, Daniel Lee Kleinman, David Hess, and Scott Frickel, "Science and Neoliberal Globalization: A Political Sociological Approach," *Theory and Society* 40/5 (2011): 505–32.

43. For instance: "The design of the Pharisees to entrap Jesus failed because he was able to transcend the dilemma they forced on him. And in so doing, Jesus was at the same time able to articulate a fundamental principle by which the disciples could chart their existence as the people of God's kingdom living in a yet imperfect world governed by secular authorities. This logion served as the beginning point of what was to be elaborated centuries later in the Lutheran two-kingdom theory. The later New Testament writers regard the ruling powers as instituted by God and as worthy of honor, faithfulness, support, and intercession (e.g., Romans 13:1–17; 1 Peter 2:13–17). It is right to render to Caesar what is Caesar's. Jesus was no Zealot or revolutionary who advocated the overthrow of the Roman government. But neither did he put priority upon loyalty to secular government. If one rendered to the state its restricted due, all the more was one to render to God his unrestricted due—the totality of one's being and substance, one's existence, was to be rendered to God and nothing less. Loyalty to Caesar must always be set in the larger context and thus be relativized by the full submission of the self to God. The bottom line for the disciple of Jesus is to 'render to God the things that are his.'" Donald A. Hagner, *Matthew 14–28* (Dallas: Thomas Nelson, 2002), 637.

possibility. And the consequence was—and is—that a rather different practice of consecration comes into play.

One implication of this historical change is that it effectively gave members of the religious community a responsibility to promote values consistent with second-tablet commandments in the extracommunal world. For modern Latter-day Saints, this kind of activism pertains not only to property, language, and sexual relationships, but, as the revised text of Doctrine and Covenants 42 makes clear, the responsibility of caring for the poor. There is an important danger here, however, to construe this kind of activism in merely social or political terms. Modern church leaders advocate involvement in society and politics, but the call to Christian discipleship cannot be construed merely in terms of social or political activism. Not only does this risk bringing political disputes into the church community, a space that is supposed to be free of contention (see 3 Nephi 11:29), but it effectively allows temporal concerns to orient spiritual concerns, rather than vice versa. Being anxiously engaged in a political or social cause is spiritually laudable, but the zeal with which these causes are pursued must be suspended by a higher spiritual awareness that recognizes the ever-present opposition between the imperfect nature of temporal concerns and the divine nature of spiritual concerns. Thus, if the spiritual is to be given primacy over the temporal, then primary spiritual concerns—such as faith and repentance—should be given primacy over political concerns. If this ordering is followed within the church, then it is possible for unity to be preserved in the midst of political activism and pluralism.

To better understand the relationship between spiritual and temporal concerns, as pertaining to specifically economic matters, it is worth considering the episode recorded in John 12 where Mary anoints Jesus with expensive ointment, after which Judas asks, "Why was not this ointment sold for three hundred pence, and given to the poor?" D. A. Carson offers the following insightful commentary on Judas's question: "The objection Judas raises has a superficial plausibility to it.... Judas displays a certain utilitarianism that pits pragmatic compassion, concern for the poor, against extravagant, unqualified devotion. If self-righteous piety sometimes snuffs out genuine compassion, it must also be admitted, with shame, that social activism, even that which meets real needs, sometimes masks a spirit that knows nothing of worship and adoration."[44] The distinction that Carson makes here between "social activism" and "worship and adoration" suggests a translation of Judas's complaint into modern economic terms, that the expensive ointment used to anoint Christ has an associated opportunity cost that cannot put the monetized value of the ointment to use in caring for the poor. Judas's question, in this sense, is blind to the spiritual aspect of Mary's act of anointing.

Judas's question can also be understood in terms of its underlying logic of economy and sacrifice. In order to anoint Jesus, the end result of actual alleviation of poverty is *sacrificed*. A sacrificial view of obedience entails a mindset of giving up something valuable for something more valuable (as discussed above regarding consecration, sacrifice, and obedience). Whatever is considered more valuable, on this logic, effectively provides extrinsic motivation for action. In contrast to this sacrificial view, a *consecrated* approach to obedience entails a wholehearted approach where actions are harmoniously aligned with desires, and behavior is intrinsically rather than extrinsically motivated.[45] From a perspective that is not merely economic, the action of anointing Jesus can be properly understood in a manner that outstrips the logic of sacrifice, and Judas's understanding of Mary's act can be inverted. The great economic value of the ointment gives Mary's act of anointing more, rather than less, significance, making it more beautiful and meaningful than if a less expensive ointment were used. It is true that a certain number of poor people might have been helped by selling the ointment and using the economic proceeds to feed the poor. However, such a view is narrow and myopic, rooted in an economically focused

---

44. D. A. Carson, *The Gospel according to John* (Grand Rapids, MI: Eerdmans, 1991), 429.

45. Alasdair MacIntyre gives a more in-depth philosophical discussion of the social implications of this difference between extrinsic versus intrinsic motivation using the language of "goods of effectiveness" and "goods of excellence" in *Whose Justice? Which Rationality?* (Notre Dame, IN: University of Notre Dame Press, 1988). In *The Retrieval of Ethics* (New York: Oxford University Press, 2011), 12–67, Talbot Brewer takes inspiration from MacIntyre and critiques the "dogmas of desire" inherent in theories of action in contemporary analytic philosophy.

interpretation of the anointing act that is blind to the diachronic, transeconomic, desire-transforming significance of Mary's act. From an economic, merely secular perspective, the anointing shows itself as an extravagant and wasteful act; but from a consecrated, religious perspective, the anointing shows itself as a spiritually meaningful act that deepens Mary's commitment to values she holds sacred.

Endemic to modern secular inquiry—and the discipline of economics in particular—is a similar tendency to ignore or devalue religious meanings.[46] Economists, for example, usually model agents' actions as manifestations of stable, exogenously given preferences, without considering interdependencies between actions and desires or the possibility of changing preferences. Similarly, political scientists typically assume an all-against-all, conflict-of-wills framework.[47] Although somewhat less guilty, the disciplines of psychology and sociology also have a tendency to embrace methodologies that value objective, empirical measurement and verification in a way that makes it difficult to capture the significance of apocalyptic texts. The possibility of repentance thus plays little to no role in social scientific inquiry. Although the scientific methods used in social science are very useful and appropriate for many practical social questions, a theological perspective must explicitly consider the possibility of change, including the feedback effects between institutions, practices, and desires. In this sense, the significance of processes of desire formation, character development, and religious rituals poses a peculiar challenge to scientific modes of statistical analysis, since such practices are deeply rooted in dynamic, subjective narratives that poorly conform to quantifiable

---

46. For a more in-depth critique of social science methodology, see Bent Flyvbjerg, *Making Social Science Matter: Why Social Inquiry Fails and How It Can Succeed Again* (New York: Cambridge University Press, 2001); and John Law, *After Method: Mess in Social Science Research* (Abingdon: Routledge, 2004). For a critique of scientism, specifically in the economics discipline, see Edward Fullbrook, ed., *Tony Lawson and His Critics* (Abingdon: Routledge, 2008).

47. See James Davidson Hunter, *To Change the World: The Irony, Tragedy, and Possibility of Christianity in the Late Modern World* (Oxford: Oxford University Press, 2010).

measurement and testing. [48] Consequently, the process of reading and interpreting scriptural texts is not only a substantive form but also a crucial methodological form of resistance to the cultivation of avaricious desires.[49]

---

48. As one group of economists expressed it, "the big questions in political economy ... are not amenable to formal modeling or traditional econometrics, but instead demand a combination of philosophical and historical reasoning." Peter Boettke, Peter Leeson, and Daniel Smith, "The Evolution of Economics: Where We Are and How We Got Here," *Long Term View* 7/1 (2008): 21.

49. The idea of fully consecrated obedience can also be related to the apocalyptic language by way of the message to the Laodiceans in Revelation 3: "I would thou wert cold or hot. So then because thou art lukewarm ... I will spue thee out of my mouth" (vv. 15–16). Although traditionally the term *lukewarm* here has been understood simply in terms moral vacillation, scholars have suggested this may refer to the local water supply and the ineffectiveness of lukewarm water when compared to hot water, which is useful for cleaning, or cold water, which is useful for drinking. To be effective, obedience requires whole-hearted fidelity, in the same manner that Jesus warned against trying to serve both God and mammon (see Matthew 6:24; Luke 16:13; 3 Nephi 13:24). In the first part of the message to the Laodiceans, John uses three titles to refer to Christ: "the Amen, the faithful and true witness, the beginning of the creation of God" (Revelation 3:14). The first title, "the Amen," seems to be a quotation of Isaiah 65:16, where God is referred to as "the God of truth" where the Hebrew word for "truth" is *aman*, the etymological root of *amen*. From this allusion to Isaiah 65, and the corresponding allusion of the third title ("beginning of the creation of God") to the subsequent verse in Isaiah ("behold, I create new heavens and a new earth," Isaiah 65:17), Jan Fekkes suggests that John is linking Christ's faithful nature with his unique manner of prefacing new teachings with the word *amen* in the phrase, "verily [*amen*] I say unto you." Fekkes, *Isaiah and Prophetic Traditions in the Book of Revelation: Visionary Antecedents and Their Development* (Sheffield: JSOT Press, 1994), 139. The allusions here to the faithful and creative nature of God, and his word, can be understood as suggesting the sense in which God's transformative, repentance-inducing word can take effect only when responded to in a likewise faithful manner. Giorgio Agamben, in his philosophical interpretation of Paul, provides a similar account of the creative power of language when spoken in faithfulness. Agamben articulates this distinction in terms of the constituting versus constituted aspects of law. See Giorgio Agamben, *The Time That Remains: A Commentary on the Letter to the Romans*, trans. Patricia Dailey (Stanford: Stanford University Press, 2005), 113–37. See also Agamben, *The Sacrament of Language: An Archaeology of the Oath*, trans. Adam Kotsko (Stanford: Stanford University Press, 2010), 54–72. Thus, one must respond faithfully—without the ineffective vacillations of a lukewarm response—in order to enjoy the creative, desire-transforming effects that genuine, whole-hearted obedience affords.

Conclusion

The revelation now comprising Doctrine and Covenants 42 recapitulates the second tablet of the Decalogue given to Moses. An important function of these laws given in ancient times was to mark a boundary between the world and the Israelite covenant community. Later, apocalyptic texts functioned as a reminder to the Israelites of the need to overcome covetous desires to obtain power or wealth. Although the violence underlying the practice of the ancient Holy War ban is difficult to understand in our modern context, the revelation given in D&C 42, when read in light of Old Testament passages such as Joshua 7 and 1 Samuel 15, draws out the overarching points of similarity between the second tablet of the Decalogue, apocalyptic texts, and the ancient practice of the Holy War ban. These similarities form an important background to LDS theological conceptions of community, consecration, and desire.

In modern secularism, church and state are conceived separately—a separation that began to emerge during the Roman Empire of Jesus's time. This secularism is reflected in most academic discourse rooted in the values of scientific rationality. Although these values of secular discourse are not antithetical to consecration, there is a tendency of these values to crowd out practices, beliefs, and institutions that sustain noncovetous desires. The religious call to care for the poor thus needs to be understood differently than the merely secular, social-scientific goal of alleviating poverty. The effective separation between spirituality and temporality promulgated by the secularism of modern society ultimately works against the interfusion of the temporal and spiritual in Latter-day Saint theology.[50] Although many varieties of secularism do

---

50. See, again, Givens, *People of Paradox*, 37–52. In light of this *uniting* of the temporal and the spiritual, Giorgio Agamben provocatively argues the etymological roots of the term *religion* come, not from *religare*, meaning "that which binds and unites the human and the divine," but from *relegere* meaning "the stance of scrupulousness and attention that must be adopted in relation with the gods ... that must be observed in order to respect the separation between the sacred and the profane." Agamben, *Profanations*, trans. Jeff Fort (New York: Zone Books, 2007), 74–75. For Agamben, the term *profanation* is used to describe what can be profitably understood in terms of a Mormon mixing of the sacred and profane in a consecrated way. To recover a positive meaning of the term *religion* based on the etymology Agamben advocates, the stark differences and

not maintain a *principled* separation of temporal and spiritual goods, even these varieties of secularism tend to enact a *practical* separation. This practical separation results in a need to foster spiritual practices, beliefs, and institutions that spiritually orient temporal concerns.

For devout Latter-day Saints, spirituality is not a Sundays-only affair. No action or practice can be safely cordoned off as having merely temporal or merely spiritual significance. But this does not mean that Mormonism must maintain an antagonistic relationship to secularism—or to capitalism. Rather, in the midst of these worldly practices, beliefs, and institutions, redemptive possibilities must be attended to. The apocalyptic resonances of Doctrine and Covenants 42, when properly understood, suggest a precarious relationship of spiritual concerns amid the tendencies of modern secularism and capitalism to appropriate spiritual language and practices to the pursuit of power and wealth. Too often, these individualistic and factional pursuits of power and wealth crowd out the pursuit of communal goods such as caring for the poor. Even when efforts to alleviate poverty are enacted by political institutions, these efforts lack the religious meaning and significance associated with a consecrated response to the needs of the poor. There is cause for celebration when progress is made in combating poverty. However, inasmuch as this progress is attained without an accompanying transformation of desire, members fail to comply with the call in the scriptures to remember and care for the poor and to consecrate their riches to them.

---

coincident soft boundaries in apocalyptic literature suggest a way forward for thinking about this fusion-separation issue.

Remnants of Revelation: On the Canonical Reading of Doctrine and Covenants 42

Joseph M. Spencer

WITH THE RECENT CHURCH-SPONSORED PUBLICATION of the Book of Commandments and Revelations and the Kirtland Revelation Book,[1] it is more likely than ever before that the average Latter-day Saint will learn that the revelations as found in the current, canonical edition of the Doctrine and Covenants have not always read as they do now. Although systematic studies of textual variations in the revelations have technically gone on for decades,[2] they are likely to increase dramatically in coming years, and more will soon be known about the revelations making up the Doctrine and Covenants—their historical context, their basic intentions, their immediate consequences—than has been known since the first generation of Mormon converts passed away.[3]

---

1. See Robin Scott Jensen, Robert J. Woodford, and Steven C. Harper, eds., *Manuscript Revelation Books*, facsimile edition, first volume of the Revelations and Translations series of *The Joseph Smith Papers*, ed. Dean C. Jessee, Ronald K. Esplin, and Richard Lyman Bushman (Salt Lake City: Church Historian's Press, 2009).

2. See especially Robert J. Woodford, "Historical Development of the Doctrine and Covenants" (PhD diss., Brigham Young University, 1974).

3. To see what kind of results are already being achieved, see examples in Steven C. Harper, *Making Sense of the Doctrine and Covenants: A Guided Tour through Modern*

Efforts to investigate textual variants in the revelations and their historical implications should be applauded, and I hope they are undertaken without reserve. Nevertheless, I will confess that I am at the same time moved by a concern that such study obscures another question that is quite as crucial as—if not actually *more* crucial than—textual and historical questions about the Doctrine and Covenants. This too easily overlooked question addresses the meaning of the revelations, not at the level of the individual passage or even section, but at the level of the entire volume. The question I thus hope will not be lost in all our textual and historical analyses of the Doctrine and Covenants is a strictly *canonical* question. To ask the canonical question is to ask about both the shape of the Doctrine and Covenants as a whole and the meaning of the individual revelation as it is situated within that whole.[4] Significantly, the shape of the whole Doctrine and Covenants has changed more drastically over the years of its publication than any single revelation contained within it during the same period of time.

I want, therefore, to ask what seems to me to be a few poignant questions about the significance of the canonical shape of the Doctrine and Covenants as we now have it. In order to stage these questions in the most forceful way possible, I want to ask them with reference to a particular revelation, the one we are collectively considering in this volume: the revelation we know today as Doctrine and Covenants, section 42. I will argue not only that this revelation has borne a *series* of canonical significations over the past two centuries but also that its *current* canonical status marks the peculiar scriptural nature of the Doctrine and Covenants as a whole as we now have it.

Revelations (Salt Lake City: Deseret Book, 2008); Mark Lyman Staker, *Hearken, O Ye People: The Historical Setting of Joseph Smith's Ohio Revelations* (Salt Lake City: Greg Kofford Books, 2009); and most recently, Michael Hubbard MacKay and Gerrit J. Dirkmaat, *From Darkness unto Light: Joseph Smith's Translation and Publication of the Book of Mormon* (Provo, UT: BYU Religious Studies Center and Deseret Book, 2015).

4. A helpful introduction to "canonical criticism" in a biblical vein can be found in James A. Sanders, *Canon and Community: A Guide to Canonical Criticism* (Philadelphia: Fortress Press, 1984).

Before the Doctrine and Covenants

At the time of the original reception of the revelation in question, the Latter-day Saints had not even begun to speak of printing, publishing, or canonizing the modern revelations of the Prophet Joseph. But because this revelation came uniquely preannounced (see D&C 38:32) and because it was very quickly accepted by the Saints generally as constituting "The Laws of the Church of Christ,"[5] what we know today as section 42 of the Doctrine and Covenants bore from the moment it was revealed a kind of protocanonical force, an authoritative status operative even before it was set to be included in an authorized book of modern scripture. Several historical details confirm this.[6] (1) The revelation was immediately coupled by the early Saints with what is now section 20 of the Doctrine and Covenants, the "Articles and Covenants" of the church. These two revelations were routinely read at conferences of the church before there was any idea of canonizing Joseph Smith's revelations.[7] (2) What is now section 42 was, significantly, the first of Joseph Smith's revelations to find its way into print. Although its first publication was actually part of an anti-Mormon effort sponsored by the apostate Symonds Ryder, the fact that he thought this particular revelation uniquely worth publishing to the world says something about its status in the early church.[8] Finally, (3) it was the third of Joseph Smith's revelations to be printed by the church itself once a press

---

5. Grant Underwood, "'The Laws of the Church of Christ' (D&C 42): A Textual and Historical Analysis," in *The Doctrine and Covenants: Revelations in Context*, ed. Andrew H. Hedges, J. Spencer Fluhman, and Alonzo L. Gaskill (Provo, UT: BYU Religious Studies Center and Deseret Book, 2008), 108.

6. Note, however, that John Whitmer recorded in his manuscript history of the church that "there were some that would not receive the Law," concluding that "the time has not yet come that the law can be fully established, for the disciples live scattered abroad and are not organized, our numbers are small, and the disciples untaught, consequently they understand not the things of the Kingdom." See Bruce N. Westergren, *From Historian to Dissident: The Book of John Whitmer* (Salt Lake City: Signature Books, 1995), 37.

7. See Woodford, "Historical Development of the Doctrine and Covenants," 527.

8. See Staker, *Hearken, O Ye People*, 295.

was established and the *Evening and the Morning Star* was launched.[9] From all these details, the protocanonical force with which the Law was received is clear. Still more, it would not be difficult to argue that it was *this* revelation in particular—especially because it was published without authorization by apostates under the title "Secret Bye Laws of the Mormonites"[10]—that turned the attention of the Saints to the possibility (or even the *necessity*) of printing, and eventually canonizing, modern revelation. But whatever the motivations, plans for the publication of the revelations—despite serious opposition from within the church[11]—were seriously underway less than a year after the Law was revealed to the church.

Once plans were formalized for what was to become the Book of Commandments, the original, protocanonical, fully normative version of the Law effectively gave way to what was intended to be a historicized (and therefore somewhat less normative) version.[12] The Book of

---

9. See "Extract from the Laws for the Government of the Church," *Evening and the Morning Star* 1/2 (July 1832): 9. This has been made readily available in Michael Hubbard MacKay et al., eds., *Documents, Volume 1: July 1828–June 1831*, vol. 1 of the Documents series of *The Joseph Smith Papers*, ed. Dean C. Jessee et al. (Salt Lake City: Church Historian's Press, 2013), 217–22.

10. "Secret Bye Laws of the Mormonites," *Painesville Telegraph*, 3/13, September 13, 1831, previously published in the Ravenna *Western Courier*, September 6, 1831.

11. See Ronald E. Romig and John H. Siebert, "First Impressions: The Independence, Missouri, Printing Operation, 1832–1833," *John Whitmer Historical Association Journal* 10 (1990): 53–56. David Whitmer apparently went so far in his opposition as to prophesy that "if they sent those revelations to Independence to be published in a book, the people would come upon them and tear down the printing press, and the church would be driven out of Jackson county." See David Whitmer, *An Address to All Believers in Christ* (Richmond, MO: David Whitmer, 1887), 54–55. The other apparently vocal opponent was William E. McLellin, whose opposition ended up in the official *History of the Church*, 1:226.

12. Plans were formalized at a conference held in Hiram, Ohio, in November 1831. The best primary source on this conference is without question Donald Q. Cannon and Lyndon W. Cook, eds., *Far West Record: Minutes of the Church of Jesus Christ of Latter-day Saints, 1830–1844* (Salt Lake City: Deseret Book, 1983), 26–32. Historical reconstructions of the endeavor to print the Book of Commandments include Peter Crawley, "Joseph Smith and *A Book of Commandments*," *Princeton University Library Chronicle* 42/1 (1980): 18–32; Romig and Siebert, "First Impressions," 51–66; and Woodford,

Commandments was to be organized chronologically, the several revelations succeeding one another in the order they had been received;
and the whole volume was to be introduced by a revealed preface
(now D&C 1) announcing that the revelations—the Law obviously
included—had been given to the Saints "in their weakness, after the
manner of their language."[13] Moreover, as if to confirm this historicizing contextualization of the Law, John Whitmer began, within days
of the decision to publish the Book of Commandments, writing an
official history of the church in which the Law was narratively contextualized in a still more striking fashion by being placed within an
unfolding history.[14] (Significantly, the same John Whitmer was one of
the three persons officially appointed to select and arrange the revelations in the Book of Commandments.)[15] These historiographically
inflected attempts at situating the revelations make clear that, within
months of its reception, the Law—despite its pretensions, *as law*, to a
kind of atemporality or at least immemoriality—became, almost by
default, chapter 44 of a book of historically situated commandments,
sandwiched between two revelations that had borne nothing like
the protocanonical status enjoyed by the Law when it was received.

"Historical Development of the Doctrine and Covenants," 21–37. Note, though, that
Robin Jensen has recently announced that it is only now, after the publication of the
Book of Commandments and Revelations, that "scholars can make an in-depth study of
[the] publishing history [of the Book of Commandments]." Robin Scott Jensen, "From
Manuscript to Printed Page: An Analysis of the History of the Book of Commandments
and Revelations," *BYU Studies* 48/3 (2009): 37.

13. See Robin Scott Jensen, Richard E. Turley Jr., and Riley M. Lorimer, eds., *Revelations and Translations, Volume 2: Published Revelations*, vol. 2 of the Revelations and
Translations series of *The Joseph Smith Papers*, ed. Dean C. Jessee, Ronald K. Esplin,
and Richard Lyman Bushman (Salt Lake City: Church Historian's Press, 2011), 17. This
revealed preface was received at the conference during which the decision to have the
Book of Commandments printed was made.

14. See Westergren, *From Historian to Dissident*. Whitmer's history has more re-
cently been made available in Karen Lynn Davidson, Richard L. Jensen, and David J.
Whittaker, eds., *Histories, Volume 2: Assigned Histories, 1831–1847*, ed. Dean C. Jessee,
Ronald K. Esplin, and Richard Lyman Bushman (Salt Lake City: Church Historian's
Press, 2012), 3–110.

15. See *History of the Church*, 1:270.

Contextualizing historicity, it seems, was set to displace strict normativity.

But, as it turned out, the Book of Commandments was never actually published because of the 1833 destruction by a mob of the printing outfit where it was in production.[16] The result was that the historicizing contextualization of the Law that would have been effected by the publication of the Book of Commandments—the initial print run for which had originally been set at ten thousand copies—did not really take place in the 1830s. Instead, and obviously in part as a response to the loss not only of the printing establishment in Zion, but of Zion itself as well, a completely different version of the Law would appear among the Saints in 1835, now in the shape of a "section" (no longer a "chapter") of the heavily institutional volume bearing the title of Doctrine and Covenants. With the 1835 publication, the normative law of 1831 and the historicized law of 1833 became at last a *fully canonical* law.[17] But this, its first real canonical presentation, is actually quite complex and deserves close attention.

Creation and closure of the canon

Full canonization of the revelations in 1835 was accompanied by a double historical cost. The revelations to be included in the volume were (1) heavily edited and (2) rearranged in an institutionally inflected, rather than strictly chronological, order. These two moves were undertaken in the wake of the massive shift, between the 1833 loss of Zion and the 1836 dedication of the Kirtland House of the Lord, from a more loosely or even democratically structured church to a church hierarchy organized for the first time around both quorums and councils.[18] The 1835

---

16. Some makeshift copies of what had been printed of the volume by the time of the destruction circulated in very limited quantities. See Crawley, "Joseph Smith and *A Book of Commandments.*"

17. The elaborate canonization ceremony by which the Doctrine and Covenants was ratified can be found in *History of the Church*, 2:244–46. The same report appears in the appendix of the 1835 edition of the Doctrine and Covenants itself.

18. On the historical effects of this near reinvention of the church's internal structure, see Marvin S. Hill, *Quest for Refuge: The Mormon Flight from American Pluralism*

publication of the Doctrine and Covenants clearly served to seal this top-to-bottom reworking of institutional Mormonism. By giving privilege of place to institutionally oriented revelations, as well as by heavily editing the revelations with an eye to the institution only then taking shape, Joseph Smith and others working on the volume wove the soon-to-be-canonized collection of revelations right into the structure of the church.

The Law was, of course, anything but exempt from these editorial procedures. Indeed, in terms of textual editing, it was—for obvious reasons—among the most drastically altered texts, particularly in its directions concerning the law of consecration and stewardship, a law that could no longer be deployed as originally written, given the loss of the Saints' lands in Zion.[19] Moreover, likely because of its erstwhile strictly normative status, the Law found its place early in the new volume as section 13, quite different from its position in the projected Book of Commandments, in which it was set to be chapter 44. Both the editorial alterations to the Law's text and the positioning of the Law as section 13 in the new volume deserve some detailed attention.

The actual placement of the Law in the 1835 Doctrine and Covenants is extremely complex. Although those who put the volume together left no explanation of the order into which the various revelations (as well as nonrevelatory materials) were put, it is possible to divine something of their thinking from an analysis of the volume itself, and such an analysis sheds a great deal of light on the changing meaning of the Law in 1835. The volume was clearly divided into two major parts: (I) the "Doctrine" (or "Theology"), consisting of the *Lectures on Faith*, and (II) the "Covenants and Commandments," consisting of the revelations and a few other items. In the latter of these two larger divisions one can further discern two major subdivisions (setting aside section 1, the revealed preface from

---

(Salt Lake City: Signature Books, 1989). On the new council system put in place in these years, see Richard Lyman Bushman, "The Theology of Councils," in *Revelation, Reason, and Faith: Essays in Honor of Truman Madsen*, ed. Donald W. Parry, Daniel C. Peterson, and Stephen D. Ricks (Provo, UT: FARMS, 2002), 433–45.

19. Since this project began, I have published a detailed study of the idea of consecration in which I provide detailed analyses of the changes made to portions of Doctrine and Covenants 42. See Joseph M. Spencer, *For Zion: A Mormon Theology of Hope* (Salt Lake City: Greg Kofford Books, 2014), 95–131.

```
┌─────────────────────────────────────┐
│      1835 Doctrine and Covenants     │
└─────────────────────────────────────┘
         ╱                    ╲
┌──────────────────┐   ┌──────────────────────────────┐
│   I. Doctrine    │   │ II. Covenants and Commandments│
│ Lectures on Faith│   │        revelations, etc.      │
└──────────────────┘   └──────────────────────────────┘
                          ╱                      ╲
┌───────────────────────────────┐   ┌───────────────────────────────┐
│ II.A. Covenants sections 2–29 │   │ II.B. Commandments sections 30–99│
│ institutionally privileged material│ │   The Book of Commandments    │
│                               │   │   incorporated into the volume │
└───────────────────────────────┘   └───────────────────────────────┘
```

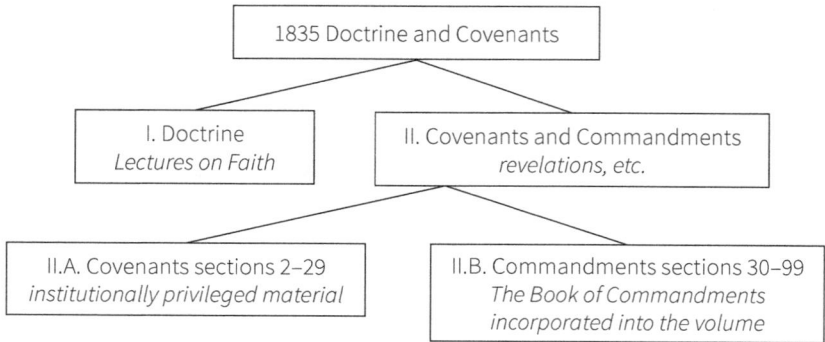

the Book of Commandments, and sections 100–102, which made up the appendix): (II.A) what was probably meant to comprise the "Covenants," consisting of revelations that seem to bear directly on questions of the organization of the church and its direct association with Zion (sections 2–29 in the 1835 edition); and (II.B) the "Commandments," consisting of all the other revelations (sections 30–99). The first of these two subdivisions (the "Covenants") is clearly privileged because of the relationship between its content and the institution the Doctrine and Covenants was meant to seal. The second (the "Commandments"), displaced to a kind of subordinate position, is something like an updated Book of Commandments (it is even strictly chronological in its internal ordering), incorporated right into the last part of the new volume.

Importantly, although one encounters some mysteries at this point, there is reason to sub-subdivide the "Covenants" subdivision of the volume such that it consists of the following: (II.A.1) a group of revelations that are clearly privileged because they deal directly and explicitly with the priesthood and the organization of the institutional church and seem to be organized in terms of institutional importance (sections 2–7); (II.A.2) a group of revelations, whose unifying theme is more difficult to ascertain but which are organized among themselves in strict chronological order (sections 8–22); and (II.A.3) another group of revelations without a clear unifying theme but organized according to an unascertainable logic (sections 23–29).[20] It is the internal ordering

---

20. That there was some kind of reason behind the separable grouping of sections 23–29 together is clear from notations made in the Book of Commandments

```
                    ┌─────────────────────────────┐
                    │      II.A. Covenants         │
                    └─────────────────────────────┘
          ┌──────────────────┼──────────────────┐
┌────────────────────┐ ┌────────────────────┐ ┌────────────────────┐
│ II.A.1 sections 2–7│ │II.A.2 sections 8–22│ │II.A.3 sections 23–29│
│institutionally ordered│ │chronologically ordered│ │   oddly ordered    │
└────────────────────┘ └────────────────────┘ └────────────────────┘
```

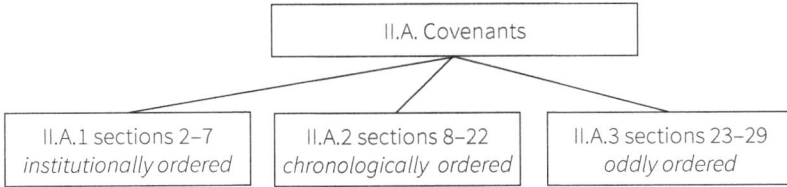

of each of these sub-subdivisions that makes clear that they should be distinguished. The Law (as section 13) falls, in the 1835 volume, within the second of these sub-subdivisions (II.A.2), that is, within the strictly chronologically ordered group of revelations, the unifying theme of which does not seem immediately obvious. This placement is what deserves close attention.

Because it was moved from the "Commandments" to the "Covenants" in the 1835 volume, the Law lost something of the immediacy of its 1833 historicization. For example, though it was preceded immediately in the Book of Commandments by what is today section 41, a revelation with clear historical connections to the Law, some forty-seven revelations separated the Law and its immediate historical predecessor in the 1835 Doctrine and Covenants. At the same time, though, because the Law found its place specifically in that sub-subdivision of the "Covenants" that is itself strictly chronological in its internal ordering, something of its historicization remained in the 1835 volume. It was immediately preceded by the revelation (now section 38) that announced the coming of the Law, and it was immediately followed by the same revelation (now section 43) that had followed it in the historically arranged Book of Commandments. It might thus be said that the Law had been removed from a kind of *absolute* historicization of the revelations (represented in the Book of Commandments) and then placed in a *relative* historicization of a select and clearly privileged string of revelations (represented by sections 8–22 of the 1835 Doctrine and Covenants). The 1835 production thus restored to the Law something of its former normativity while nonetheless retaining

---

and Revelations. John Whitmer there numbers these eight revelations (employing the numbers 1–8) in precisely the order they appear in the 1835 Doctrine and Covenants. See Jensen, Woodford, and Harper, *Manuscript Revelation Books*, 159.

something—however limited—of its historicity. It was thus possible at once (1) to allow aspects of the revelation that could have been described, by 1835, as *dated* to fall away from normativity into historicity and nonetheless (2) to retain as normative what of the revelation might still be taken as bearing on the behavior and activity of the Saints.

This same double aim can be detected as well in the actual changes made to the text of the revelation. Not only was it torn from its place in an absolute chronological ordering of the revelations in 1835, it was also reworked at the level of the text in such a way that its actual wording would have been out of place in February of 1831 when it was originally received. This reworking, it is clear, was intended to allow the revelation to slip into the past while nonetheless drawing from its erstwhile normative power certain guiding principles for the church. Detailed studies of the changes made to the Law in 1835 have long been available,[21] and I will for the most part here simply defer to them, postponing any detailed discussion of the changes until I turn to the 1876 edition of the Doctrine and Covenants, where the details of the changes made to the revelation become more relevant to my purposes in this paper.

Before turning from the 1835 Doctrine and Covenants, though, it is worth inserting a note because the many alterations made to Joseph Smith's revelations in 1835 have been a point of concern for some Latter-day Saints. While I understand the motivation behind such

---

21. Grant Underwood traces the most important changes in what is now section 42 in some detail in Underwood, "'Laws of the Church of Christ,'" 114–34. A comparison of the two "systems" of consecration thus outlined, one in 1831, the other in 1835, is nicely provided in the form of two charts in Lyndon W. Cook, *Joseph Smith and the Law of Consecration* (Provo, UT: Grandin Book, 1985), 19, 32. These changes in the system of stewardship have been traced historically in many publications. Among the most widely influential are, apart from Cook's study, Leonard J. Arrington, Feramorz Y. Fox, and Dean L. May, *Building the City of God: Community and Cooperation among the Mormons* (Urbana: University of Illinois Press, 1992); and Mario S. DePillis, "The Development of Mormon Communitarianism, 1826–1846" (PhD diss., Yale University, 1960). Again, I might mention my own more recent study of these changes: Spencer, *For Zion*, 95–131.

concerns, I believe them to be unnecessary, if not simply misguided.[22] Latter-day Saints today should take comfort in the fact that the Saints of 1835 were quite aware of and remained unbothered by the changes made to the revelations: the earlier, unmodified versions of many of the revelations had been made widely available in the church's newspapers; many Latter-day Saints had personal copies of the original revelations made before any version of the revelations appeared in print; and unofficial copies of the Book of Commandments were in limited circulation from 1833. Moreover, the fact that changes were made in the process of canonization is anything but surprising in light of what especially nineteenth- and twentieth-century biblical scholarship has discovered about scriptural texts. Canonical (or "final") shape is given to scriptural texts only over time, and the "original" texts are inevitably altered in the process of shaping what becomes the canonical text. This fact has driven what is now a two-hundred-year-old debate in biblical scholarship. It serves no one's interests to insist dogmatically that the canonical and the original texts are identical. The fact is that there are many differences, and we can actually trace and then reflect on those differences. The task of the faithful Saint, it seems to me, is decide what those changes have to teach us.

So much, then, for the shape of the Law in its first fully canonical presentation in 1835. But, significantly, the story of the Doctrine and Covenants did not end in 1835. The volume actually was, for about a decade, an *open* canon, primarily because the Seer was still alive. There was, therefore, little surprise when a handful of revelations— most received after 1835—were added to the volume in 1844. But the addition of these revelations, particularly because they came accompanied by an announcement of the martyrdom of Joseph and Hyrum

---

22. Unfortunately, some have compounded the problem by using a statement in the minutes for a conference meeting on November 8, 1831 ("Resolved by this conference that Br Joseph Smith Jr correct those errors or mistakes which he may discover by the holy Spirit while receiving the revelations reviewing the revelations & commandments & also the fulness of the scriptures") to suggest that all changes made to the revelations for the 1835 Doctrine and Covenants were reversions from inadvertent mistakes in copying and printing to the original received text. This simply is not the case. For the minutes of the meeting, see Cannon and Cook, *Far West Record*, 29.

Smith that was intended "to seal the testimony" of the book,[23] effectively *closed* the canon, giving it what would be its definitive shape for a full generation. No significant changes would be made to the Doctrine and Covenants until 1876.

As if to confirm the closing of the canon and to establish definitively the distance between history and canon, the church began to publish for the first time Joseph Smith's official history in the same years that the 1844 edition of the Doctrine and Covenants was in preparation, was published, and was being initially promulgated.[24] Orson Pratt emphasized this point a decade later when he wrote that "Joseph, the Prophet, in selecting the revelations from the Manuscripts, and arranging them for publication, did not arrange them according to the order of the date in which they were given, neither did he think it necessary to publish them all in the Book of Doctrine and Covenants, but left them to be published more fully in his History."[25]

This closure of the canon was, however, set in motion less in 1844 than in 1835. Then it was that the distance between canon and history, between the canonical and the original, was first put on display. The open/closed canon of the 1830s and 1840s would not be called into question until 1876, when the same Orson Pratt found himself with the task of completely reworking the Doctrine and Covenants. Because the version of the Doctrine and Covenants that took shape only in 1876 is more or less the same read today, and particularly because it fixed the canonical shape of the Law as it is still today found in LDS scripture, the 1876 edition of the Doctrine and Covenants deserves the closest attention of all.

---

23. Now section 135 of the Doctrine and Covenants. Note that the same announcement speaks of Joseph having "sealed his mission and his works with his own blood" (D&C 135:3). The closing of the canon was structurally tied to the closing of Joseph's mortal life.

24. The history was published in serial fashion in both the *Times and Seasons* (in Nauvoo) and the *Millennial Star* (in Liverpool) starting in 1842.

25. Orson Pratt, "Restoration of the Aaronic and Melchisedek Priesthoods," *Millennial Star* 19 (April 25, 1857): 260. I owe this reference to David Whittaker.

Complicating the canon

The 1876 reorganization of the Doctrine and Covenants marked, in many ways, a return to the original program of the Book of Commandments. The revelations were—apparently at the behest of Brigham Young himself—returned from their 1835/1844 institutional arrangement to their 1833 chronological organization. The Historian's Office Journal from the time of Orson Pratt's work on the volume reads: "By the counsel of President B. Young, Elder Pratt has divided the various revelations into verses and arranged them for printing, according to the order of the date in which they were revealed."[26] (The only *intentional* exceptions to this chronological arrangement in 1876 were also exceptions in the planned 1833 Book of Commandments. The revealed "preface" and the revealed "appendix" to the Book of Commandments, now sections 1 and 133, retained their places at the beginning and the end of the volume, though they were revealed in 1831.) Thus a kind of rehistoricization of the revelations was accomplished, a reassignation of the revelations to an absolute chronology.

As it turned out, though, this historicization of the revelations was actually *more* complete than that undertaken in the effort to publish the Book of Commandments. In addition to reorganizing the revelations chronologically, Orson Pratt, assigned to undertake the reorganization of the volume, added a number of sections that had never appeared in the Doctrine and Covenants. Most of these were not technically revelations but excerpts from Joseph Smith's history—whether accounts of angelic visitations or items of instruction drawn from Joseph's teachings.[27] Given what Pratt himself had said in 1857

---

26. Quoted in Woodford, "Historical Development of the Doctrine and Covenants," 76. Breck England, apparently without justification, seems to suggest that the decisions about rearrangement were Pratt's own: "Orson also arranged the *Doctrine and Covenants* chronologically; his was the first edition to contain 136 sections in the order given by revelation." See England, *The Life and Thought of Orson Pratt* (Salt Lake City: University of Utah Press, 1985), 255.

27. Pratt's primary source for these selections—as well as for the historical details he worked into the section headings for revelations already in the Doctrine and Covenants before 1876—was clearly Joseph Smith's history as published in the *Millennial*

about Joseph Smith's intention to reserve some of his revelations and teachings for his published history, it is clear that he (Pratt) intended the 1876 edition to function as a kind of hybrid of the Doctrine and Covenants and the *History of the Church*—to be, that is, an as-narrativized-as-possible compilation of the revelations. (In this regard, it is significant that Orson Pratt was already pressing for the exclusion of the not-at-all-historically oriented *Lectures on Faith* soon after he had completed the reorganization of the volume for the 1876 edition. This fact suggests that he already saw the reworking of the Doctrine and Covenants as leaving little room for "theological lectures or lessons" that would soon be excluded from the volume. Indeed, it is likely best to see the 1921 removal of the lectures more as the completion of—rather than supplementary to—the reorganizing efforts Pratt undertook with the Doctrine and Covenants.)[28]

It is difficult to know exactly what is implied by this restoration of Joseph Smith's revelations to a strictly chronological order and to a quasi-historicized format. Was the reorganization meant to flatten the structural hierarchicization of the revelations worked out in the 1835 edition? Or was it perhaps a kind of confession, at the point of the passing of the first generation of the church, that Joseph's revelations had subtly shifted from their originally strong normativity to a kind of subordinate status vis-à-vis the "living" authority of the church hierarchy? Was it tied to an implicit recognition that the serially published *History of the Church* would never be a popular read, both because of its length and because of its heavily documentary nature? Was it perhaps even meant to organize a kind of prehistory of the cooperative organizations and communities that were proliferating at the very time of the publication of the newly organized edition of the volume?[29] Or was it connected to the enormous reorganization of the church's institutional structure that occupied the last years of Brigham Young's life?

Star. I plan to argue this systematically in a paper titled: "Narrativizing the Revelations of Joseph Smith: Orson Pratt and the 1876 Edition of the Doctrine and Covenants."

28. See Woodford, "Historical Development of the Doctrine and Covenants," 85–88.

29. See Arrington, Fox, and May, *Building the City of God*, 111–54; and especially D&C 136.

Whatever the answers to these likely unanswerable questions, the Law—what had canonically stood for four decades as section 13 of the Doctrine and Covenants—now became section 42 of the reorganized volume, definitively placed within a basically absolutized chronology. Gone are the fine distinctions that divided, subdivided, and sub-subdivided the 1835 volume. But as soon as one takes a detailed look at what had finally become section 42, one immediately recognizes that there is something problematic about this restored chronological ordering. When Pratt restored Joseph Smith's revelations to the "original" order, he did not restore them to their original wording; only one of the two reshapings undertaken in 1835—the altered placement in the volume, but not the altered text itself—was controverted. The textual changes that had been made in the process of canonizing the revelations for the institutionally oriented 1835 collection pass over without even so much as a comment into the deinstitutionalized and rehistoricized compilation that is the 1876 edition. The vital consequence of this decision—if it was, in fact, a question at all of decision[30]—is that the revelations have been, since 1876, at once both clearly *chronological* in their organization and yet profoundly *anachronistic* in their actual content.

Section 42 is exemplary on this point. Though it was finally placed firmly between sections 41 and 43 because it was, according to the section heading of 1876, "given ... February 9th, 1831," it is actually, at the level of the text, a combination of *two* originally distinct revelations, one received indeed on February 9, 1831, and the other received on February 23, 1831, that is, *after* sections 43 and 44. These

---

30. It is clear that Orson Pratt did not use many (if any) manuscript sources in the preparation of the 1876 edition of the Doctrine and Covenants. He seems not even to have consulted the Book of Commandments. His principal—and almost only—source was clearly the history as printed in the *Millennial Star*. Again, I will be arguing for these details in "Narrativizing the Revelations of Joseph Smith." That Pratt did not consult the manuscript sources is, however, somewhat ironic, because it seems clear that Pratt was aware of them. See Jensen, "From Manuscript to Printed Page," 43, 51. And he was, during the time of his work on the 1876 edition, the official Church Historian, ensuring his full access to—and likely his full awareness of—the manuscript resources held by the church. See England, *Life and Thought of Orson Pratt*, 260.

two revelations had been published as distinct communications both in early church periodicals and in the Book of Commandments.[31] They had only been combined into a single revelation for the first time with the publication of the 1835 edition of the Doctrine and Covenants, their being joined together apparently motivated by obvious intentional thematic connections between them.[32] Nonetheless, precisely because those connections are mediated by a revelation received between what was originally its two parts—namely, what is now section 43—the assignment of all of what is now section 42 to the date of February 9, 1831, is ultimately anachronistic.

Of course, one should not fault Pratt for failing to separate the two original revelations in his work on the 1876 volume, especially given the fact that they were not separated in the printed version of Joseph Smith's history which Pratt followed so meticulously.[33] And, frankly, what ultimate difference do the two weeks between February 9 and February 23, 1831, make? But, as it turns out, this stitching together of two originally distinct revelations is the least of the anachronisms of section 42 as published in 1876. Indeed, a whole series of anachronisms appears, not surprisingly, in the verses that had been so heavily edited in the process of producing the canonized version of the revelation for

31. See the helpful chart in Underwood, "'Laws of the Church of Christ,'" 111.

32. As Underwood points out, the Symonds Ryder manuscript of the Law makes clear that there was a historical connection between the two revelations stitched together in 1835. It describes the material from February 23, 1831, as being about "How the Elders of the church of Christ are to act upon the points of the Law given by Jesus Christ to the Church." This language clearly draws on the language of what is now D&C 43:8, which commanded the elders of the church to "instruct and edify each other, that ye may know how to act and direct my church, how to act upon the points of my law and commandments, which I have given" (see the Book of Commandments, chapter 45, verse 8 for the earlier version of this wording: the elders were to "note with a pen how to act, and for my church to act upon the points of my law and commandments, which I have given"). See Underwood, "'Laws of the Church of Christ,'" 111–12. For the Ryder manuscript, see Michael Hubbard MacKay et al., eds., *Documents, Volume 1: July 1828–June 1831*, vol. 1 of the Documents series of *The Joseph Smith Papers*, ed. Dean C. Jessee et al. (Salt Lake City: Church Historian's Press, 2013), 245–56.

33. See their publication as a single revelation in "History of Joseph Smith," *Millennial Star* 14 Supplement (1852): 57–60.

the 1835 edition of the Doctrine and Covenants—all the most glaring of these anachronisms deal, crucially, with the law of consecration and stewardship. A few of them might be mentioned specifically: verse 31 makes reference to high priests, an office and order of the priesthood that would not be introduced into the church until some six months after the Law was given; verse 33 sets forth the order of the bishop's storehouse in terms that would not have made sense until the organization of the United Firm a year later; and, most anachronistic of all, verse 34 mentions the high council, which would not be organized until 1834![34] Anyone reading the Doctrine and Covenants closely—particularly if he or she lends an attentive eye to the historical or narrative framework the volume itself imposes—must inevitably begin to wonder what is at work in the consistent appearance of such anachronisms.

The importance of this last point must not be missed. Though they had technically been present from 1835 (this is what I called above the inevitability of a tension between canon and history), these anachronisms only come to light authentically and on their own terms when the revelations are officially arranged in a chronological, rather than institutional, order. While readers of the 1835 edition of the Doctrine and Covenants *might* have been able to spot the kinds of anachronisms I have here pointed out, they would have done so *only* by dismissing the canonical structure of the volume itself—by dismissing the obviously institutional arrangement of the revelations in favor of what ultimately would have been, with regard to the text, an alien historiographical concern. But because the actual canonical shape of the Doctrine and Covenants after 1876 is itself driven by a historiographical concern, it is the faithful, rather than the dismissive, reader of the Doctrine and Covenants who is now drawn to the problem of anachronism in the revelations.[35]

---

34. These anachronisms can all be detected without reference to nonscriptural sources. That high priests were not ordained until June of 1831 is stated clearly in the (1981) section heading for section 52; that the order of the bishop's storehouse is out of place in 1831 is immediately apparent in light of section 78; and the fact that the high council did not exist before 1834 is made abundantly clear in section 102.

35. Though, because I am dealing with the Doctrine and Covenants and because that volume is a very different book from the Book of Mormon, I will differ here from

What one ultimately finds, then, in the Doctrine and Covenants after 1876—and every reader of the Doctrine and Covenants today is a reader of the Doctrine and Covenants after 1876—is a problematizing of the very notion of canon. Whereas the 1835 edition of the Doctrine and Covenants functions as a canon in a very classical sense, according to which canon is effectively at odds or in tension with history as such, the 1876 edition functions as a canon in a quite distinct fashion. The 1876 volume refuses to hold canon and history at such a distance from each other. At the same time, however, it must be noted that neither does it simply fuse history and canon in a straightforward manner, as, perhaps, the Book of Commandments would have done had it been completed and circulated widely. Had the Book of Commandments been completed and received as canonical by the church, it would have been an instance of *canonizing the historical*, of giving authoritative status to the history. The 1876 volume, on the other hand, can be said to effect a *historicizing of the canonical*, both refusing to revert from the canonical rendering of the revelations (as these were fixed in 1835) *and* nonetheless reorganizing the canonical revelations in a strictly historical order.

What one finds in the 1876 edition of the Doctrine and Covenants, then, is not exactly a reopening, after 1844, of the modern canon. Though various documents have been added to the Doctrine and Covenants since 1876,[36] it is not clear how open the Doctrine and Covenants can ultimately be said to be. Rather, what Orson Pratt's reworking of the volume seems to have accomplished was a double fracturing, at once a fracturing of the idea of canonicity (a setting of one notion of canon against another) and a fracturing of the idea of history (a setting of one notion of history against another). It is as if it has, since 1876,

Adam S. Miller's work on how to interpret the theological significance of anachronism. See his fantastic essay on anachronism in the Book of Mormon: "Messianic History: Walter Benjamin and the Book of Mormon," in *Discourses in Mormon Theology: Philosophical and Theological Possibilities*, ed. James M. McLachlan and Loyd Ericson (Salt Lake City: Greg Kofford Books, 2007), 227–45.

36. Sections 137 and 138, as well as both official declarations, have been added to the volume since 1876. In addition, as mentioned in an earlier note, the *Lectures on Faith* were dropped from the volume in 1921.

become a part of reading the Doctrine and Covenants to begin piecing together the details of early Mormon history.[37] At the same time, though, through the classically canonical (that is, 1835) shape of the revelations in the Doctrine and Covenants, one is also bound to take the text at its current word, regardless of how it might "originally" have been dictated.

The Doctrine and Covenants today, then, confronts the reader not so much with revelations as with *remnants* of revelations, with fragments of revelatory events, texts suspended between their at once canonically historical and historically noncanonical status.[38] This is perhaps particularly true of the Law, and so of our curious position before the law of consecration as contained in the Doctrine and Covenants. To be faithful in this instance means that we can neither settle for a kind of historiographical fundamentalism, embracing some precanonical "original" meaning of the Law drawn from the historical sources, nor feel comfortable taking the canonical text solely at its nonhistorical word, dismissing the force of a divinely orchestrated history that has produced us.[39] Our task, it seems, is—interpretively as well as practically—to give ourselves to a God whose communicated truths are reducible neither to history nor to an absolute divine word, to act in strong accordance with the curiously Mormon belief that truth—God's truth—is at once eternal and yet sorted out historically.

In a word, it may well be that consecration itself is precisely the difficult work of refusing to compromise either what "God once was" or what "God now is."

---

37. This is made particularly clear when section headings refer the reader directly to the seven-volume *History of the Church*.

38. This understanding of the way the Doctrine and Covenants positions its reader between or among what appear to be several competing positions is, in many ways, reminiscent of what I have called the four discourses of Mormonism. See Joseph M. Spencer, "The Four Discourses of Mormonism," *BYU Studies* 50/1 (2011): 4–24.

39. This is the position I take also in *For Zion*, attempting to defend the normative force of the final form of the law of consecration as laid out in D&C 42. See Spencer, *For Zion*, 133–57.

Bibliography

Ackerman, Bruce, and Anne Alstott. *The Stakeholder Society*. New Haven: Yale University Press, 1999.

Agamben, Giorgio. *Profanations*. Translated by Jeff Fort. New York: Zone Books, 2007.

——. *The Sacrament of Language: An Archaeology of the Oath*. Translated by Adam Kotsko. Stanford: Stanford University Press, 2010.

——. *The Time That Remains: A Commentary on the Letter to the Romans*. Translated by Patricia Dailey. Stanford: Stanford University Press, 2005.

Andrews, Dan, and Andrew Leigh. "More Inequality, Less Social Mobility." *Applied Economics Letters* 16/15 (2009): 1489–92.

Arrington, Leonard J., Feramorz Y. Fox, and Dean L. May. *Building the City of God: Community and Cooperation among the Mormons*. 2nd ed. Chicago: University of Illinois Press, 1992.

Aquinas, Saint Thomas. *The Summa Theologica of St. Thomas Aquinas*. 5 vols. New York: Benziger Brothers, 1948.

Austin, John. *The Province of Jurisprudence Determined and the Uses of the Study of Jurisprudence*. Indianapolis: Hackett, 1998.

Bauckham, Richard. "Revelation." In *The Oxford Bible Commentary*, edited by John Barton and John Muddiman, 1287–1305. New York: Oxford University Press, 2001.

Benson, Ezra Taft. *Teachings of Ezra Taft Benson*. Salt Lake City: Bookcraft, 1988.

————. *A Witness and a Warning: A Modern-day Prophet Testifies of the Book of Mormon.* Salt Lake City: Deseret Book, 1988.

Bergera, Gary James. *Conflict in the Quorum: Orson Pratt, Brigham Young, Joseph Smith.* Salt Lake City: Signature Books, 2002.

Berman, Harold J. *Law and Revolution: The Formation of the Western Legal Tradition.* Cambridge, MA: Harvard University Press, 1983.

Boettke, Peter J., Peter T. Leeson, and Daniel J. Smith. "The Evolution of Economics: Where We Are and How We Got Here." *Long Term View* 7/1 (2008): 14–22.

Boyce, Duane. "Do Liberal Economic Policies Approximate the Law of Consecration?" *FARMS Review* 21/1 (2009): 197–213.

Brague, Rémi. *The Law of God: The Philosophical History of an Idea.* Translated by Lydia G. Cochrane. Chicago: University of Chicago Press, 2007.

Bryson, Phillip J. "In Defense of Capitalism: Church Leaders on Property, Wealth, and the Economic Order." *BYU Studies* 38/3 (1999): 89–107.

Bushman, Richard Lyman. *Joseph Smith, Rough Stone Rolling: A Cultural Biography of Mormonism's Founder.* New York: Alfred A. Knopf, 2005.

————. "The Theology of Councils." In *Revelation, Reason, and Faith: Essays in Honor of Truman Madsen,* edited by Donald W. Parry, Daniel C. Peterson, and Stephen D. Ricks, 433–45. Provo, UT: FARMS, 2002.

Butler, Trent. *Joshua.* Edited by D. W. Watts. Vol. 7 of *Word Biblical Commentary.* Waco, TX: Word Books, 1983.

Cannon, Donald Q., and Lyndon W. Cook, eds. *Far West Record: Minutes of the Church of Jesus Christ of Latter-day Saints, 1830–1844.* Salt Lake City: Deseret Book, 1983.

Cannon, George Q. "Opposition to the Saints, and Its Cause." In *Journal of Discourses,* 24:38–50.

Carlson, Allan C. *Third Ways: How Bulgarian Greens, Swedish Housewives, and Beer-Swilling Englishmen Created Family-Centered Economies—and Why They Disappeared.* Wilmington, DE: ISI Books, 2007.

Carson, D. A. *The Gospel according to John.* Pillar New Testament Commentary. Grand Rapids, MI: Eerdmans, 1990.

The Catechism of the Catholic Church. Retrieved from http://www
.vatican.va/archive/catechism/p3s1c2a3.htm, April 25, 2016.

Charry, Ellen T. "'A Sharp Two-Edged Sword': Pastoral Implications of
Apocalyptic." In *Character and Scripture: Moral Formation, Community, and Biblical Interpretation*, edited by William P. Brown,
344–60. Grand Rapids, MI: Eerdmans, 2002.

Cook, Gene R. *Teaching by the Spirit*. Salt Lake City: Deseret Book,
2000.

Cook, Lyndon W. *Joseph Smith and the Law of Consecration*. Provo,
UT: Grandin Book, 1985.

———. *The Revelations of Joseph Smith: A Historical and Biographical Commentary of the Doctrine and Covenants*. Salt Lake City:
Deseret Book, 1985.

Cook, Stephen L. *Prophecy and Apocalypticism: The Postexilic Social
Setting*. Minneapolis: Fortress, 1995.

Corbin, Henry. *History of Islamic Philosophy*. Translated by Liadain
Sherrard and Phillip Sherrard. London: Kegan Paul International,
1993.

Crawley, Peter. "Joseph Smith and *A Book of Commandments*." *Princeton University Library Chronicle* 42/1 (1980): 18–32.

Crosby, John F. *The Selfhood of the Human Person*. Washington, DC:
Catholic University of America Press, 1996.

Davidson, Karen Lynn, Richard L. Jensen, and David J. Whittaker,
eds. *Histories, Volume 2: Assigned Histories, 1831–1847*. Vol. 2 of
the Histories series of *The Joseph Smith Papers*, edited by Dean C.
Jessee, Ronald K. Esplin, and Richard Lyman Bushman. Salt Lake
City: Church Historian's Press, 2012.

DePillis, Mario S. "The Development of Mormon Communitarianism,
1826–1846." PhD diss., Yale University, 1960.

Dunn, James D. G. *The Theology of Paul the Apostle*. Grand Rapids,
MI: Eerdmans, 1998.

England, Breck. *The Life and Thought of Orson Pratt*. Salt Lake City:
University of Utah Press, 1985.

Faulconer, James E. "Rethinking Theology: The Shadow of the Apocalypse." In *Faith, Philosophy, Scripture*, 109–36. Provo, UT: Neal A.
Maxwell Institute, 2010.

Faulring, Scott H., ed. *An American Prophet's Record: The Diaries and Journals of Joseph Smith*. Salt Lake City: Signature Books, 1989.

————. "An Examination of the 1829 'Articles of the Church of Christ' in Relation to Section 20 of the Doctrine and Covenants." *BYU Studies* 43/4 (2004): 57–91.

Fekkes, Jan, III. *Isaiah and Prophetic Traditions in the Book of Revelation: Visionary Antecedents and Their Development*. Sheffield, UK: JSOT Press, 1994.

Firmage, Edwin Brown, and Richard Collin Mangrum. *Zion in the Courts: A Legal History of the Church of Jesus Christ of Latter-day Saints, 1830–1900*. Urbana: University of Illinois Press, 1988.

Fuller, Lon. *The Morality of Law*. Rev. ed. New Haven: Yale University Press, 1969.

Gadamer, Hans-Georg. "The Problem of Historical Consciousness." In *Interpretive Social Science: A Reader*, edited by Paul Rabinow and William M. Sullivan, 103–60. Berkeley: University of California Press, 1979.

Gedicks, Frederick Mark. "The 'Embarrassing' Section 134." *Brigham Young University Law Review* 2003/3 (September 2003): 959–72.

————. "The Integrity of Survival: A Mormon Response to Stanley Hauerwas." *DePaul Law Review* 42/1 (Fall 1992): 167–73.

Givens, Terryl L. *People of Paradox: A History of Mormon Culture*. New York: Oxford University Press, 2007.

Gordon, Sarah Barringer. *The Mormon Question: Polygamy and Constitutional Conflict in Nineteenth-Century America*. Chapel Hill: University of North Carolina Press, 2002.

Habermas, Jürgen. "Israel and Athens, or to Whom Does Anamnestic Reason Belong? On Unity in Multicultural Diversity." In *Liberation Theologies, Postmodernity, and the Americas*, edited by David Batstone, Eduardo Mandieta, Lois Ann Lorentzen, and Dwight N. Hopkins, 243–52. New York: Routledge, 1997.

Hagner, Donald A. *Matthew 14–28*. Edited by Ralph P. Martin and Lynn A. Losie. Vol. 33B of *Word Biblical Commentary*. Dallas: Word Books, 2002.

Hall, Kermit L. *The Magic Mirror: Law in American History*. New York: Oxford University Press, 1989.

Harper, Steven C. "'All Things Are the Lord's': The Law of Consecration in the Doctrine and Covenants." In *The Doctrine and Covenants: Revelations in Context*, edited by Andrew H. Hedges, J. Spencer Fluhman, and Alonzo L. Gaskill, 212–28. Provo, UT: BYU Religious Studies Center, 2008.

————. *Making Sense of the Doctrine & Covenants: A Guided Tour through Modern Revelations.* Salt Lake City: Deseret Book, 2008.

Heathcote, Jonathan, Fabrizio Perri, and Giovanni L. Violante. "Unequal We Stand: An Empirical Analysis of Economic Inequality in the United States, 1967–2006." *Review of Economic Dynamics* 13/1 (2010): 15–51.

Hegel, G. W. F. *Elements of the Philosophy of Right.* Edited by Allen W. Wood. Translated by H. B. Nisbet. New York: Cambridge University Press, 1991.

Hill, Marvin S. *Quest for Refuge: The Mormon Flight from American Pluralism.* Salt Lake City: Signature Books, 1989.

Hills, John, Tom Sefton, and Kitty Stewart, eds. *Towards a More Equal Society? Poverty, Inequality and Policy since 1997.* Bristol: Policy Press, 2009.

Hinckley, Gordon B. *Teachings of Gordon B. Hinckley.* Salt Lake City: Deseret Book, 1997.

Howard-Brook, Wes, and Anthony Gwyther. *Unveiling Empire: Reading Revelation Then and Now.* Mary Knoll, NY: Orbis Books, 1999.

Hunter, James Davison. *To Change the World: The Irony, Tragedy, and Possibility of Christianity in the Late Modern World.* New York: Oxford University Press, 2010.

Jensen, Robin Scott. "From Manuscript to Printed Page: An Analysis of the History of the Book of Commandments and Revelations." *BYU Studies* 48/3 (2009): 19–52.

Jensen, Robin Scott, Richard E. Turley Jr., and Riley M. Lorimer, eds. *Revelations and Translations, Volume 2: Published Revelations.* Vol. 2 of the Revelations and Translations series of *The Joseph Smith Papers*, edited by Dean C. Jessee, Ronald K. Esplin, and Richard Lyman Bushman. Salt Lake City: Church Historian's Press, 2011.

Jensen, Robin Scott, Robert J. Woodford, and Steven C. Harper, eds. *Manuscript Revelation Books.* Facsimile edition. First volume of the Revelations and Translations series of *The Joseph Smith Papers*, edited by Dean C. Jessee, Ronald K. Esplin, and Richard Lyman Bushman. Salt Lake City: Church Historian's Press, 2009.

Journal of Discourses. 26 vols. Liverpool: various publishers, 1854–1886.

Kanter, Rosabeth Moss. *Commitment and Community: Communes and Utopias in Sociological Perspective*. Cambridge, MA: Harvard University Press, 1972.

Kearl, James R., and Clayne Pope. "The Church in the Secular World." Paper presented at Brigham Young University, Provo, UT, 1975.

Kierkegaard, Søren. *Purity of Heart Is to Will One Thing*. Translated by Douglas V. Steere. San Francisco: HarperOne, 1956.

Lucas, James W., and Warner P. Woodworth. *Working toward Zion: Principles of the United Order for the Modern World*. Salt Lake City: Aspen Books, 1996.

MacIntyre, Alasdair. *Whose Justice? Which Rationality?* Notre Dame, IN: University of Notre Dame Press, 1988.

MacKay, Michael Hubbard, and Gerrit J. Dirkmaat. *From Darkness unto Light: Joseph Smith's Translation and Publication of the Book of Mormon*. Provo, UT: BYU Religious Studies Center and Deseret Book, 2015.

MacKay, Michael Hubbard, Gerrit J. Dirkmaat, Grant Underwood, Robert J. Woodford, and William G. Hartley, eds. *Documents, Volume 1: July 1828–June 1831*. Vol. 1 of the Documents series of *The Joseph Smith Papers*, edited by Dean C. Jessee, Ronald K. Esplin, Richard Lyman Bushman, and Matthew J. Grow. Salt Lake City: Church Historian's Press, 2014.

Marlett, Jeffrey. "Harvesting an Overlooked Freedom: The Anti-Urban Vision of American Catholic Agrarianism, 1920–1950." *U.S. Catholic Historian* 16/4 (Fall 1998): 88–108.

Marquardt, H. Michael. *The Joseph Smith Revelations: Text and Commentary*. Salt Lake City: Signature Books, 1999.

Marx, Karl. *Selected Writings*. Edited by Lawrence H. Simon. Indianapolis: Hackett Publishing, 1994.

May, Dean L. "The Economics of Zion." *Sunstone*, August 1990, 15–23.

May, William E. "Contemporary Perspectives on Thomistic Natural Law." In *St. Thomas Aquinas and the Natural Law Tradition:*

Contemporary Perspectives, edited by John Goyette, Mark Latkovic, and Richard Myers, 113–56. Washington, DC: Catholic University of America Press, 2004.

McConville, Gordon. "Joshua." In *The Oxford Bible Commentary*, edited by John Barton and John Muddiman, 158–75. New York: Oxford University Press, 2001.

Miller, Adam S. "Messianic History: Walter Benjamin and the Book of Mormon." In *Discourses in Mormon Theology: Philosophical and Theological Possibilities*, edited by James M. McLachlan and Loyd Ericson, 227–45. Salt Lake City: Greg Kofford Books, 2007.

Millet, Robert L. "Joseph Smith's Translation of the Bible: A Historical Overview." In *The Joseph Smith Translation: The Restoration of Plain and Precious Things*, edited by Monte S. Nyman and Robert L. Millet, 23–47. Provo, UT: BYU Religious Studies Center, 1985.

Moore, Kelly, Daniel Lee Kleinman, David Hess, and Scott Frickel. "Science and Neoliberal Globalization: A Political Sociological Approach." *Theory and Society* 40/5 (2011): 505–32.

Nibley, Hugh. *The World and the Prophets*. Edited by John W. Welch, Gary P. Gillum, and Don E. Norton. Salt Lake City: Deseret Book and FARMS, 1987.

Niditch, Susan. *War in the Hebrew Bible: A Study in the Ethics of Violence*. New York: Oxford University Press, 1993.

Novak, David. "Secularity without Secularism: The Best Political Position for Contemporary Jews." *Hedgehog Review* 8/1–2 (Spring–Summer 2006): 107–15.

Oaks, Dallin H. "Teaching and Learning by the Spirit." *Ensign*, March 1997, 6.

Oman, Nathan B. "'The Living Oracles': Legal Interpretation and Mormon Thought." *Dialogue: A Journal of Mormon Thought* 42/2 (Summer 2009): 1–19.

Pratt, Orson. "Restoration of the Aaronic and Melchisedek Priesthoods." *Millennial Star* 19 (April 25, 1857): 257–60.

———. "Union of Spirit and Sentiment, Etc." In *Journal of Discourses*, 7:371–76.

Quinn, D. Michael. *The Mormon Hierarchy: Origins of Power*. Salt Lake City: Signature Books, 1994.

Robinson, Stephen E. "Nephi's Great and Abominable Church." *Journal of Book of Mormon Studies* 7/1 (1998): 32–39.

Romig, Ronald E., and John H. Siebert. "First Impressions: The Independence, Missouri, Printing Operation, 1832–1833." *John Whitmer Historical Association Journal* 10 (1990): 51–66.

Romney, Marion G. "Welfare Services." *Ensign*, November 1975, 124.

Sanders, James A. *Canon and Community: A Guide to Canonical Criticism.* Philadelphia: Fortress, 1984.

Sider, Ronald J. *Rich Christians in an Age of Hunger: Moving from Affluence to Generosity.* Nashville: Thomas Nelson, 2005.

Smith, Christopher C. "The Inspired Fictionalization of the 1835 United Firm Revelations." *Claremont Journal of Mormon Studies* 1/1 (2011): 15–31.

Smith, Joseph, Jr. *History of the Church of Jesus Christ of Latter-day Saints.* Edited by B. H. Roberts. 7 vols. Salt Lake City: Deseret Book, 1971.

Smith, Rodney K. "James Madison, John Witherspoon, and Oliver Cowdery: The First Amendment and the 134th Section of the Doctrine and Covenants." *Brigham Young University Law Review* 2003/3 (2003): 891–940.

Snow, Lorenzo. "United Order, Etc." In *Journal of Discourses,* 19:341–50.

Sorenson, A. Don. "Being Equal in Earthly and Heavenly Power: The Idea of Stewardship in the United Order." *BYU Studies* 18/1 (1977): 100–117.

Spencer, Joseph M. *For Zion: A Mormon Theology of Hope.* Salt Lake City: Greg Kofford Books, 2014.

———. "The Four Discourses of Mormonism." *BYU Studies* 50/1 (2011): 4–24.

Staker, Mark Lyman. *Hearken, O Ye People: The Historical Setting for Joseph Smith's Ohio Revelations.* Salt Lake City: Greg Kofford Books, 2009.

Staker, Susan, ed. *Waiting for World's End: The Diaries of Wilford Woodruff.* Salt Lake City: Signature Books, 1993.

Stein, Stephen J. "American Millennial Visions: Towards a Construction of a New Architectonic of American Apocalypticism." In *Imagining the End: Visions of Apocalypse from the Ancient Middle*

East to Modern America, edited by Abbas Amanat and Magnus Bernhardsson, 187–211. New York: I. B. Tauris, 2012.

Stern, Philip D. "Isaiah 34, Chaos, and the Ban." In *Ki Baruch Hu: Ancient Near Eastern, Biblical, and Judaic Studies in Honor of Baruch A. Levine,* ed. Robert Chazan, William W. Hallo, and Lawrence H. Schiffman, 387–400. Winona Lake, IN: Eisenbrauns, 1999.

Sternberg, Meir. *The Poetics of Biblical Narrative: Ideological Literature and the Drama of Reading.* Bloomington: Indiana University Press, 1987.

Taylor, Charles. "Language and Human Nature." In *Human Agency and Language: Philosophical Papers 1,* 215–47. New York: Cambridge University Press, 1985.

Taylor, John. *The Government of God.* London: Latter-day Saints' Book Depot, 1852.

Thompson, Leonard L. *The Book of Revelation: Apocalypse and Empire.* New York: Oxford University Press, 1990.

Tyler, Tom R. *Why People Obey the Law.* Princeton, NJ: Princeton University Press, 2006.

Underwood, Grant. "'The Laws of the Church of Christ' (D&C 42): A Textual and Historical Analysis." In *The Doctrine and Covenants: Revelations in Context,* edited by Andrew H. Hedges, J. Spencer Fluhman, and Alonzo L. Gaskill, 108–41. Provo, UT: BYU Religious Studies Center and Deseret Book, 2008.

Vanderbilt, Tom. *Traffic: Why We Drive the Way We Do (and What It Says about Us).* New York: Alfred A. Knopf, 2008.

Weber, Max. *The Vocation Lectures.* Edited by David Owen and Tracy B. Strong. Translated by Rodney Livingstone. Indianapolis: Hackett, 2004.

Westergren, Bruce N., ed. *From Historian to Dissident: The Book of John Whitmer.* Salt Lake City: Signature Books, 1995.

Wheelwright, Philip. *Metaphor and Reality.* Bloomington: Indiana University Press, 1962.

Whitmer, David. *An Address to All Believers in Christ.* Richmond, MO: David Whitmer, 1887.

Widtsoe, John A. *Joseph Smith: Seeker after Truth, Prophet of God.* Salt Lake City: Bookcraft, 1951.

Wilcox, S. Michael. *What the Scriptures Teach Us about Prosperity.* Salt Lake City: Deseret Book, 2010.

Wolff, Hans. *Roman Law: An Historical Introduction.* Norman, OK: University of Oklahoma Press, 1951.

Woodford, Robert J. "The Articles and Covenants of the Church of Christ and the Book of Mormon." In *Sperry Symposium Classics: The Doctrine and Covenants*, ed. Craig K. Manscill, 103–16. Provo, UT: BYU Religious Studies Center and Deseret Book, 2004.

——. "The Historical Development of the Doctrine and Covenants." PhD diss., Brigham Young University, 1974.

Wright, Erik Olin. *Envisioning Real Utopias.* London: Verso, 2010.

Yorgason, Ethan. "No Grounds for Conversation: The Regional Construction of Fundamental Differences between Mormonism and Socialism." *Antipode: A Radical Journal of Geography* 34/4 (2002): 707–29.

Young, Brigham. "The Order of Enoch, Etc." In *Journal of Discourses*, 16:8–12.

——. "Salvation." In *Journal of Discourses*, 1:1–6.

Contributors

ROBERT COUCH is assistant professor of finance at Earlham College. His research interests include questions pertaining to the confluence of finance, ethics, and theology.

RUSSELL ARBEN FOX is professor of political science at Friends University, a small nondenominational college in Wichita, Kansas. He has published articles and reviews on early American nationalism, German romantic philosophy, communitarianism, public education, Confucian political and moral theory, Utah socialism, Mormon politics, and bicycling.

JEREMIAH JOHN is associate professor of politics at Southern Virginia University. He has degrees from Hampden-Sydney College and the University of Notre Dame.

NATHAN B. OMAN is a professor at William & Mary Law School. He was educated at Brigham Young University and Harvard Law School. He lives in Williamsburg, Virginia, with his wife, two children, and a black Lab named Duncan.

JOSEPH M. SPENCER is visiting assistant professor of ancient scripture at Brigham Young University. He is the author of *An Other Testament*, *For Zion*, and *The Vision of All*.

KAREN E. SPENCER is an independent scholar. She studied humanities at Brigham Young University and has presented her work at the annual meetings of the Association of Mormon Scholars in the Humanities in addition to participating in the Mormon Theology Seminar.